CALL SIGNS

CALL SIGNS

RICH DINKEL

iUniverse LLC
Bloomington

Call Signs

iUniverse books may be ordered through booksellers or by contacting:

iUniverse LLC
1663 Liberty Drive
Bloomington, IN 47403
www.iuniverse.com
1-800-Authors (1-800-288-4677)

ISBN: 978-1-4759-7391-4 (sc)
ISBN: 978-1-4759-7392-1 (hc)
ISBN: 978-1-4759-7390-7 (ebk)

Library of Congress Control Number: 2013901972

Printed in the United States of America

iUniverse rev. date: 07/24/2013

Contents

This book is dedicated to

Those Who Didn't Come Home

May they rest in peace

Introduction

Marine and Navy Aviators are gregarious folks. They enjoy getting together and partying in a hearty manner—together. When they are away from their flying machines, they try to clear their minds for a little bit of cranial R&R (Rest and Relaxation), so that they can be sharp enough to do whatever has to be done now, that day, the next day, and, the next, anon.

As our Naval Aviation folks pack up and board their Carriers with their flying machines, on occasion we Marines are invited (. . . ah, read, ordered) to show our skills when we deploy to places unknown with our Navy comrades.

Reflecting back on my twenty-plus years flying in the Corps, I can say that I have been blessed by having an understanding wife, supporting kids, and an entire Corps of supportive elders, advisors, wingmen, and those absolutely wonderful and amazing "Green Amphibious Monsters, who have no fear, because they <u>ARE</u> fear!"

Please allow me give you a bit of a running start by giving you a bit of who, what, when, where and by whom.

Now, a Call Sign is a form of pseudonym (read "fictitious name"), which is used by a person, or sometimes, a group. History is filled with many pseudonyms. They have been used to hide an individual's real identity, such as with writers' pen names, graffiti "artists" tags, a resistance fighter's or terrorists' nom de guerre, or a truck driver's or computer geek's handle. Stage Names are also used as something which better matches their on-stage personae, such as "Sting," "Soupy Sales," or "Madonna," for example.

Let's begin by defining the some of the necessity, usefulness, and scope of a Call Sign.

The Call Signs of today are a form of pseudonym (as a scholar might call it), which means "A fictitious name used by a person, or sometimes, a group." History is filled with pseudonyms. They have often been used to hide an individual's identity, such as in writers' pen names, graffiti artists' tags, a resistance fighter's or terrorist's nom de guerre, a truck driver's or computer geek's handle, anon. Stage names are also used as something that better matches their on-stage personae, as in "Sting," "Goober," "Gomer," "Zorro," "Ape" etc. In some cases, pseudonyms can be adopted because of a cultural or organizational tradition group.

A Pen Name (or a "nom de plume") is a pseudonym which was adopted by authors often as a way to conceal their identity. A great example might be Samuel Clemens' writing under the pen name of Mark Twain. Another successful author, Charles Dodgson, wrote novels under the pen name of Lewis Carroll, while others, (such as Harold Robbins, for example) that used several different "nom de plumes," and wrote novels under their changing pen names, or "nom de plumes."

So, as you can see, "nom de plumes" have been around and in common use for quite some time. During all this, the French did not want to be "up staged," so they rolled out their "nom de guerre," which is French for "Names of War," or "War Names." It is said that recruits of the French Foreign Legion quickly adopted this idea, so as to break away from their past lives. That practice hid their identities quite well, and protected their families from any kind of reprisal, and, perhaps, giving them a viable dissociation from their former "domestic" life.

Now, remember: The French Foreign Legion was populated predominately by convicts who were "eligible" to go into the French Foreign Legion.

In addition to these pseudonyms, there are the Stage Names of actors and singers, as well as other entertainers' stage names. "Kiss" and "Zorro" immediately come to mind.

When used by a radio operator, the pseudonym can be referred to as a "Handle." You will get a lot more exposure and examples regarding Call Signs throughout this entire book!

Since I flew fast jets for about 20 years in the Marine Corps, I will try to give you the "feel" of what it is like to be racing across the terrain, going at approximately the speed of stink, with your hair on fire, and out-maneuvering all the Bad Boys out there who don't "like" us, our cohorts, or our Country. Actually, those "Bad Boys" seem to hate ANY American, for that manner, and would just love to shoot us down . . . . but, while doing all this, we were having the best fun that we possibly could have with our clothes on! And, in addition,—get this—we are actually getting PAID to do it!

Tactical aviation might be seen as a risky business in the eyes of pedestrians and/or non-tactical aviators. While that view has not been completely eradicated, today's fighter/

attack flying machines (such as the F/A-18 Hornet) are absolutely awesome! Their performance, built-in safety provisions, electronic capabilities, radar, and pilot visibility is second to none. The on-board computer is WAY faster and smarter than R2D2! Some of our other jets can hover, take off vertically, and land on their own, in a vertical manner, while others can be launched off the bow of an aircraft carrier, and recovered in the cross-deck wires at the stern.

These very expensive and amazingly capable aircraft are flown by sharply skilled professionals, who train and re-train constantly to ensure that their thought processes, aeronautical skills, and a wide range of capabilities of their jet are always honed to a razor's edge.

The knowledge that they must attain and retain can be considered as encyclopedic. To them, however, it is just part of the "love affair," and they wouldn't change it for the world . . . . .well . . . . .maybe not when getting ready to launch on some ink-dark night with no moon, with a pitching and/or rolling deck, sea water coming over the bow, and no divert fields within his fuel load limits. It is a personal (but never articulated) "Gulp" every time you do something like that, BUT you DO it . . . . . and you don't whine about it. You do it anyway, and hope the "shooter" (launch controller) was paying attention!!! When you get back to the ship, you align yourself and your wingmen for the Break (The normal way to come back to the ship). You turn hard to port (left) while abeam the turn around to port, and descend (into "the groove") which puts you at the stern (back) of the Carrier (IF you did it right), and then come aboard by catching one of the four Cross Deck wires with your Tail Hook (which you MUST deploy if you want to come aboard), and "Trap" by your "Hook," by snaring one of four Cross-Deck Pendants. When you catch your breath, you will need to immediately taxi clear of the cross-deck pendants, so as to allow the guy right behind you, so he could land as well. Once on the deck, you automatically morph, and return back into the person you really are, once again, and no longer behave as the acutely well-tuned robotic, "take no prisoners" man/woman that you just were a very short time ago. In this manner, a human-machine system can be fielded and honed to take on all comers, in all climes, day or night, in any weather, and—most importantly—WIN.

Now, this is important: In the Naval/Marine Corps Services, it is really "Bad Form" for an individual to select/adopt/ use a Call Sign which he or she, has bestowed upon one's self without the blessing of their seniors and/or squadron mates. Doing something such as that approaches "Prima donna-ism!" If this should ever occur, senior squadron mates (and especially Commanding Officers) will probably go far out of their way to "award" those self-blessed Call Sign holders with a—let's just say—a "DIFFERENT" Call Sign.

Perhaps, something you may not "love," such as Drifty, Ugly, Barf, Dufus, Crash, Oops!, One Way, Wrong Way, Dirt, Filthy, etc., etc. The potential selection options are as many as a human can possibly imagine!!

Now, there are (at least) two kinds of Call Signs:

1. Formal/Institutional, and
2. Tactical

FORMAL/INSTITUTINAL:

Call Signs are normally derived and assigned by "Higher Headquarters." These Formal Call Signs are generally long, extended, and difficult to pronounce. Lower-level units will normally have longer Call Signs than its parent Command, and the further you go down the "food chain," the longer the Call Sign becomes (in most current applications). History has proven that long-duration Call Signs decrease cockpit <u>S</u>ituational <u>A</u>wareness (SA to aviators). In so doing, this greatly compromises the individual pilot's ability to accomplish six or seven things at once (in a Hornet), while flying along at (Let's just say LOTS) of knots at 200 feet AGL (<u>A</u>bove <u>G</u>round <u>L</u>evel), at night, with no moon, while still keeping tactical positioning on each other (i.e. In a two-or four-jet formation) for defense, and precisely navigating along the pre-planned route! (Note: As you can clearly see, this very high-workload often tends to expand due to multi-tasking.) Pilots often refer to this phenomenon as "The Ole Helmet Fire" for the person who is alone in the cockpit!

On the other hand, "Tactical Call Signs" must (by necessity) be brief, crisp, and immediately understandable, so that the pilot of the single-seat jet can safely accomplish the myriad of things he must do—all at once—while down there just above the dirt/water at a "sporty" clip, on a moonless night, while precisely navigating so as to arrive on Target, on Time. Accordingly, the savvy tactical aviator can help solve the dilemma by shortening his/her "On the Air" Time by using a BRIEF tactical/personal call sign—i.e. "Dog," "Fang," "Boomer, or "Gazelle"—which have only one or two syllables.

Tactical Aviation is often described as very risky business in the eyes of pedestrians, ground pounders, wives, and non-tactical aviators. Today's fighter and attack aircraft can take-off and land on a runway, hover and/or take off and land on their own in a vertical manner (just about anywhere), while others can be shot off the bow (front) of an aircraft carrier, and recovered in the cross-deck pendants at the stern (rear) of the ship. In order to do any of this sort of flying, a pilot must have steely eyes with 20/20 vision (or better), quick, cat-like reflexes, exceptional common sense, and last, but not least, he or she must have deep and wide knowledge of every system aboard the aircraft.

When we look back over the years, and discuss who did what to whom, why, how, and when we did it, and to what degree and level of success . . . . It is theoretically POSSIBLE that our memories could recall events which might possibly have been just a tad "bigger, faster, meaner, and more dangerous" than they actually were at the time. Accordingly, I have made a valiant effort to separate and quantify "Absolute Truth" from the "Sea Stories" within this book, and have eliminated most of . . . . (well, some of) . . . . the latter.

Now, having said all of that, I must admit that on some nights, when there is no moon, and you are far away from land, in deep water, with no other place to land, and when the ship pitches (moves up and down) ten to fifteen feet, with white water coming over the bow, and rolling (listing back and forth) at, say, 20 or so degrees, I discovered that "some folks" are not sure that they are really "cut out" for this kind of flying.

It's kind of like learning to ride your first two-wheeled bicycle—but at a much higher altitude and a considerably faster pace!

Chapter 1

Notso

It was a beautiful, clear day in southern Texas when NOTSO passed his "Safe for Solo" flight check. He was thrilled to have passed that important test flight! To his surprise, he was immediately asked by his instructor if he would like to go for his first <u>SOLO</u> flight . . . . RIGHT NOW! He wasted no time, and immediately responded with a hearty "YES, SIR!"

In what took less than 45 minutes, Second Lieutenant Bright was taxing out of the chocks, heading for the runway to fly his first SOLO flight in a jet. He was immediately cleared for Take Off, and spent about 45 minutes just doing anything that <u>HE</u> wanted to do! He felt like he was the most "COOL" guy in the Cosmos! He wanted to get some more landing practice, so he decided to start heading home.

He chose to take just a little more time to simply enjoy himself, amidst the beautiful weather. He chuckled to himself when it popped into his head that this kind of weather is referred to by the "Weather Guessers" as CAVU (Clear And Visibility Unlimited), and he sure did have one that day.

As he scanned his gauges, he noticed that he had a little extra gas left, so he headed for home to do a few "Touch and Goes." (Meaning: Land, then add power, climb, call the Tower for permission, & turn down-wind, until at the 180 degree position, where he simultaneously let down and turned toward the runway, and land (for a Full Stop) or do another "Touch and Go," so as to repeat the cycle, again, depending upon his fuel state.

As he approached the field, he was advised by the Control Tower that a runway change was just beginning (due to a wind shift) and the Tower told him to "loiter" and circle at 5,000 feet (AGL), in a left-turn, and wait until they can finish the Runway Change. He appropriately said, "Roger," complied with his instructions, and took his position at the appropriate altitude. After an unusually long time, some other fliers arrived on the scene and joined him in "The Stack" at their appropriately assigned altitudes. When he checked his gauges, he noticed a "Red Light" on his fuel gauge, which was his signal that it was time for him to land—SOON—because he was just about out of fuel. His pesky little red light was doing its job, by bugging him, and reminding him that it's time to be on the ground. He started becoming a bit nervous, so he called the

Tower, and declared "Low Fuel" (Which was exactly what he was supposed to do.)

The Tower came back, and asked, "Are you declaring an Emergency?"

Now, I have flown long enough to know that asking a "brand new" pilot if he/she wants to declare an Emergency, he/she should feel OBLIGATED to declare an Emergency because that is what he/she is SUPPOSED to do!

This controller, however, got his bowels in an uproar, and made a "big deal" about it! Well . . . . So, what do you think happens next?

The young lad was cleared to descend into the pattern and was Cleared To Land. He flew a a great pass and flew "The Ball right on "the rails." As he flew over the ramp he was having to "Ease Gun" (pull the throttle back) more than he ever had to before, and he then touched down on the centerline of the runway . . . . and immediately the all Hades broke loose!

HIS LANDING GEAR WERE STILL UP AND LOCKED!!

He told me, years later, that he was, "Just along for the ride, after he realized what was happening!"

After being knocked around in the cockpit a bit, and hearing many very loud and foreign sounds, the machine very ungraciously came to a halt just off the left side of the runway. As he was shutting down and hastily evacuating from his jet (just as he had been taught), he noticed "about a hundred" pieces of what used to be his flying machine . . . . It was spread all over the runway, and out in the weeds, too!

He was out of and away from the jet in record time. When the Crash Crew and a Medical Van arrived at the scene, they quickly noted the Tower that airplane parts were, ah . . .

EVERYWHERE!

Our pilot was put into the Medical Van immediately by the Corpsmen. The Flight Surgeon was waiting for him in the van, and, as soon as he sat down, he noticed a Sailor lying in the van with a very bloody bandage wrapped around his head. Well, our hero got a little panicky; because he immediately thought that he had landed on top of this guy!

What REALLY happened was that, when the "Meat Wagon" hurriedly left the parking lot for the runway with sirens blaring, the Sailor turned out to be a Corpsman who was racing to catch up with the Meat Wagon, who stumbled and fell on his head! Although he was bleeding profusely, the Meat Wagon guys pulled him in, and rapidly continued to the crash site.

On their way to the crash site, they discovered that he was not as bad as they had originally thought. Captain Bright later related that he thought that he had somehow landed on this guy on the runway, and injured him, and it worried him a lot more than landing with his landing gear up!

He also added, "As I was "cooling down, I soon realized that I now had to put on my "dancing shoes" because I am going to have a lot more to worry about back in the Squadron."

Our intrepid aviator, still in shock, was immediately taken to the Flight Surgeon's Dispensary, as required by regulations, although he kept telling them that he was just fine. When they finally released him, he went back to his Squadron Ready Room in the ambulance. He knew what was going to happen next, and he wanted to take his mind off that thought. A million thoughts were cycling around in his "Brain Housing Group" in an amazingly rapid rate!" Once in the Ready Room, everyone was very glad to see him. He was, in one piece, so everyone was thrilled . . . . EXCEPT ONE PERSON . . . the Commanding Officer, who, not so politely "invited" him to his office, and told him to be sure to "Close the door as you come in." Needless to say, our intrepid aviator did not expect—nor did he get—to be offered any coffee or good will.

After the obligatory loudly spoken, fire from the nostrils, red faced, one-way "discussion" the CO calmed down a bit, took a deep breath, and said, "What you did today was <u>NOT VERY BRIGHT</u>, Captain," as the CO rudely ushered him out of his office.

Well, Captain Bright was very down-trodden. When he got down to the Ready Room, all the other pilots wanted to know what happened. By this time, our hero must have been quite embarrassed by the whole thing, so he just replied to his buddies that, "The Skipper told me that I was "not so bright."

And—in my professional opinion—THE GREATEST CALLSIGN OF ALL TIME WAS BORN! That is:

NOTSO BRIGHT!

What a guy! He <u>still</u> acts just like he always did, back in his younger days. I proudly tell "Notso" stories to anyone who will listen!

A while ago, Colonel Notso asked me if I was planning to write about any of his "Bar Tricks." I had to fess up and tell him that I had <u>forgotten</u> about that "expertise" he used to have. Within a few seconds, it all came floating back to me, so, while I am at it, here is another (mostly true) story about my favorite Mentor.

I met Colonel Notso again in the Officers' Club at Marine Corps Air Station, El Toro in Southern California, during a Friday night Happy Hour. As I walked in the door of the Club, I headed over toward the bar, and saw a balding little guy setting up drinks and making some deals with the many Officers at the Bar. I shied over toward the crowd, to see Colonel Notso doing a "Barker" routine, and Marines were putting money on the bar to bet that Colonel Notso "couldn't do IT. I was not sure or what they all were doing, until one of my buddies arrived, and proceeded to tell me that "Notso" is doing another one of his "things." Tonight, it looks like he's betting that he can drink a full Long Neck bottle of beer while hanging upside down on the bar, without using his hands, and drink all the beer with his teeth without spilling any of it. You will like it—it's really cool.

Well, we pushed and wiggled our way through the masses toward the bar, and by the time we worked ourselves into a spot where we could see, we (naturally) needed some beer, so we pushed further up the bar, joked with Colonel Notso, got our beer, and bet that he COULD do IT (whatever "IT" was), and then . . . . he was about ready to do . . . ah, "IT" . . . and, YES, I know what you are thinking, and yes, you are correct—I was young (and a bit gullible) in those days!

Since I worked so hard to get close enough to see what was really going on, I grabbed another two beers for us with which to watch the show properly—whatever "it" was. Well, I got my wish in short order, because I heard the shout, "All Bets In!"

The money was then passed to the Bar Tender for safe-keeping, and Notso pushed back the crowd, put the full long neck beer bottle on the floor right next to the bar's foot rail. He then jumped up, hung by this calves on the bar, and facing away from the bar, did a "reverse push-up," and grabbed the beer bottle with his teeth, turned it skyward, chugged all the beer in the bottle (while he was up-side down), placed the bottle where he had picked it up (with his teeth), and when it was empty, asked folks to give him some room, and—when they cleared the way—he did a backward flip to his feet. It was absolutely <u>amazing</u>! To say that I was impressed would have been WAY under-stated!

What a guy!!

From that day on, he became my favorite Devil Dog, Full Bird Colonel!

Semper Fi, Sir

I believe.

Chapter 2

"Animal"

In the mid-60s, I learned to always "assume" that the "Animal" was pulling another of his "tricks" on me with all his stories! He can make up a story . . . himself . . . right out of thin air, down to the smallest detail, and then, five or ten years later, also remember (what I assumed was BS) that he fed to us, down to those SAME smallest details! The "Animal"—AKA Al Ransom—has been kind enough through the years to give me some of his historical savvy, and, most importantly, his friendship in helping me in pulling this book together, as well. "Thanks for your help, Big Guy!"

In the early '60s, there was no such thing as a personal "Tactical Call Sign." Every fast-moving "Naval Aviator" (Yes, Marines fall into that category), in any given Squadron, pilots/RIOs used their assigned Squadron Call Sign (Such as: Bugger, Huh?, Blade, Dixieland, for example). Back in the "Good Ole Days" when men were men, and sheep were afraid, and a Lineal Number in that specific Squadron was assigned, from top to bottom. For example, the Squadron Commander's Call Sign would/could be "Blade One," and his Executive Officer would be assigned "Blade Two," and so on, down the lineal list. That system worked pretty well in the days when the aviators were sent to a Squadron, and then stayed in that unit for a long time, normally deploying en-mass, as a singular unit.

Well "Someone" decided (Pause: Did anybody ever figure out who "Someone" WAS?) that the system was not working terribly well, however, at about that time, "Someone" decided that Squadrons should train, then send individuals—one by one—for Off-Shore assignments. In a few years, that methodology was discarded, in favor of unit rotations . . . again.

The historically significant advent of encrypted communication capabilities has greatly enabled the war fighter to communicate with almost anyone in the world. Some other cultural things, however, remain the same. By that, I mean, things such as the famous and infamous "3-Man Lift."

I have absolutely no idea who invented the 3-Man Lift, nor do I know when it was debuted . . . . I have been told, however, that it was a Navy or a Marine Fighter Pilot on a very long voyage (or deployment) who had absolutely nothing better to do than to think this one up. But, I digress . . . .

The 3-Man Lift usually takes place in some sort of saloon, bar, picnic, or whatever—just use your imagination. (I saw one "performed" on the Beach on the Jersey Shore. Yup—I will <u>always</u> remember that one . . . . I was the "Lucky One" who was targeted, but I digress . . . .)

The 3-Man Lift has been known to occur at a Squadron Party, Officers' Club (well, maybe NOT <u>these</u> days), a Private Party, or just about anywhere else where there is copious quantities of beer (or other beverages) available. (PS: Urine, in any manner, shape, or form is NOT allowed to be inside of 100 feet from the actual "lift." That would be a severe "Domi Domi"—meaning "A VERY BAD THING" in Japanese. The "Lift" is usually associated with a "special" event (. . . . be it a good event, or yet another super stupid, reckless, &/or REALLY DUMB action), or—frankly—just acting like a big, red, flaming, ahh, animal that might be taken for a donkey!

This is how the 3-Man Lift is <u>supposed</u> to be done.

For starters, it begins by 2 or more guys loudly arguing about something semi-believable such as:

- "Ya know, I can dead lift half a TON"
- "Can <u>YOU</u> lift 3 men by yourself? No?? Well, I can."
- "Well, I can lift three men . . . all by myself!
- Or feel free to pick <u>your own</u> BS . . . .

The "<u>Barker</u>" (who runs the show) initially begins by saying something to the tune of: "OK, then, let's just find out how strong you Marines REALLY are! I am looking for his two more—ah—"participants." I want an average weight of about (Pick a number)"

Now, *this* is the "gaming" part . . . . TWO of the three folks who will be" lifted" are <u>In On The Game</u>. So, they will be placed in the front and the rear as the "human weight." When the Barker says sit down on the floor, the "Target" is then strategically positioned between the two big guys who are "in on" what's REALLY going to happen.

When they get the three people they want, the Lifter then warms up by doing some calisthenics, and "participants" slither over to the bar for all/any kind of liquid (beer, booze, water, etc.), and are returning back to the "lift" area (which is preferably tile or cement).

As the three men are being tightly positioned together—interlocked like a 3-Man "sled," the Barker is ensuring that the "<u>Target</u>" is between the two people who know what is going to happen, and what their roles are. When the Barker sees that all the other people/bystanders have gathered their "liquid of choice," he positions the three participants appropriately, checks that all bets are in, and encourages that the people move in as tightly together as possible—so that the "Lifter" can have enough room to actually lift these guys up. (Yeah . . . . Right).

When all is ready, the "Barker" slowly barks: 1 . . . . 2 . . . . and on 2 the front guy rolls out forward, the back guy rolls backward, and everybody else pours their liquids on top of the "Target."

I have to tell you . . . . a well-orchestrated "Three Man Lift" is a thing of BEAUTY!

Mister "Lucky One" then gets dry . . . . at least a little bit . . . . and he also gets a free cold beer slapped in his hand!

I personally met The Animal early in my Marine Corps career, and had the pleasure of learning many "<u>good</u>" as well as "<u>other</u>" things from him. Although he tells his many stories best while sitting on a bar stool for several hours, I was able to pin him down long enough to get his stories into this book.

Note: I had to kill a lot of brain cells during my quest to quantify what you are reading at this very instant! No sane guy should ever go "bar hopping" with the Animal, unless he can drink as much as The Animal can.

The precise origin of Al's "Animal" Call Sign is unknown, however, it can be simplified by one lady's response to some of his antics, by saying, "Oh, Al . . . . You are <u>SUCH</u> an <u>ANIMAL</u>!" So many people were calling him an animal, he just accepted "Animal" as a Call Sign. In addition, "Animal Al," has a nice "ring" to it." (Think they will buy any of this, Animal?)

Well, I can tell story upon story regarding my wildest and craziest mentor," Animal Al. He has been called a LOT of things, and most of them were actually really GOOD things.

So, when he went back to the States, the Blue Angels were just gearing-up to fly F-11F Tigers. Whoever was trying out for The Blues would have to get checked out in the Tiger, and they all would do it at NAS Beeville, in The Animal's Squadron. The Animal was assigned to be their personal Instructor, and "Beans," Craig (USMC), was one of those guys who was in the squadron. He had been touted as a really good "stick."

"Bean's" specific training was to get spooled up to become the Solo Pilot for the Blue Angels (Navy Demonstration Team), ASAP! The Animal was assigned to check out all the new guys in the F-11. Beans assured The Animal that they would have fun doing this.

As they launched and climbed, The Animal was pointing out . . . . SILENCE! Whoops!

The Animal just had a "Flame Out"!

With a bit of "pucker factor" (with his butt securely sucked down on the seat of his jet), he went through his formal Re-Light procedures. Pause. Pause. Pause . . . . and the Boooorrr sound indicated that the engine was spooling up, and everything was coming back on-line, albeit slowly. He never said a word to his wingman, (who was glued to the Dog's right wing), and as the engine spooled up, he gave him the head nod for a "power up," and they continued the mission. JUST LIKE IT NEVER HAPPENED!

NOTE: Years ago, Fighter Pilots would simply say that they had to just, "Cool It" because the jets and motors of that time were not as "reliable" as the wonderful engines of today.

Well, Animal's ground job was the OIC (Officer In Charge) of the Power Plants Shop (Read: ENGINES), so he had his Chief (Enlisted Naval Semi-Big-Wig) pull the aircraft into the hangar for a formal engine check . . . just in case.

Now, as you might guess, there are many, many more Sea (and other kinds of) Stories about the Animal . . . . and, believe it or not, just about ALL of them are very likely to be TRUE! All those who know him well realize that he is definitely a "One of a kind kinda guy!

So, after thinking about The Animal and his capers, I think that you readers deserve just one more "Animal" story . . . .

In 1961, The Animal was transferred to MCAS El Toro, in Southern California. On a CAVU (Clear And Vision Unlimited) day, he was flying the Dash 2 slot in a four-plane formation, traveling back to Base after a 2 vs. 2 ACM (Air Combat Maneuvering) sortie. They were just crossing over Dana Point, at 3000 feet. Don Stiver was the flight leader, and he had just pumped the Section over (i.e. numbers 3 and 4) to cross into right side, in echelon. The Animal, flying the number two slot, slid in a little closer to the Leader so that the flight would look "squared-away" when they entered "The Break" (i.e. Peel off, one at a time, slow down, and drop the landing gear and the flaps, then execute the Landing Check List, expecting to hear the "Cleared to land," from the Control Tower.) NOTE: On the ground, people are looking up at the jets to "critique" the execution of the "Break" . . . . a pedestrian's way of "evaluating" the capabilities of the Gents flying the jets).

Note: The Break (in anticipation of landing) was developed during WWI, so as to alleviate the enemy's capability to sneak up behind an airplane that was slowing down to land.

As Al slipped closer to the Leader, he noticed something that was "International Orange and White" in his peripheral vision, and called it out on the radio!

Dash 3 (Larry Reiman) yelled, "Look Out!" . . . . but, no one heard anything other than, "Out!"

Dash 3 and 4 went off to the left, and Al pulled hard to the right, in heavy buffet. At the same time, the Leader went past the left front wing of an F-4D, and Al realized that he was heading right for it, too! Al ended up taking six inches off the F-4D's right wing!

Al pulled up, and noted that pieces were flying off HIS jet, and dash 4 transmitted,

"AL . . . . <u>EJECT!</u>"

And the Leader yelled, "Dash Two—RAISE YOUR SPEED BRAKES! All Al heard was "Speed Brakes, but he was already raising them as the Leader was called. The Leader sent 3 and 4 home. Al piped up, and said, "I can go in the Break, Boss. I'm fine."

The Leader just said, "SHUT UP AL, and hold it nice and steady; I'm going to take a look at your jet."

The Leader crossed back and forth under Al's "broken" jet, looking hard for tell-tail "dings" . . . . or worse. (Note: At that juncture, Al didn't know that he had "participated" in a mid-air collision!) Al tried to talk to his Leader, but he didn't answer, so Al switched his radio over to the Control Tower frequency. The first thing he heard was, "MAYDAY! MAYDAY! MAYDAY! I HAVE HAD A MID-AIR COLLISION."

Al thought, "Oh, no. Someone had a Mid-Air!"

It was the A4D talking. He was yelling, and trying to get a clearance into Runway 34 Left. Immediately, another voice came on the air, and he is talking about something related to the wing of another aircraft, and that aircraft had a two-foot hole in his left aileron. It hit Al like a Brick S__T House! It suddenly came clear to Al that it was HE that they were talking about! That was also when (he says) he FROZE UP, but just for a moment or two. Well, they slowed down and discovered that whenever Al slowed below 175 knots, his left wing would lose lift, and begin to stall.

Accordingly, they decided to make a straight-in approach at 180 knots, with his arresting hook down. Al caught the Morest Gear (that's one Cross Deck pendant, strung across the runway, and attached to about 150 feet of large, linked anchor chain on each side of the runway, which had been put "in battery" on Runway 34 Right, without further ado. Upon touchdown, he rolled into the Morest Gear, came to a stop, and experienced no further complications. At Happy Hour that afternoon, Al acted "a bit like an Animal" by verbally attacking the poor, defenseless, wimpy little R4D pilot (Note: If I didn't tell you before, Al is a pretty <u>BIG</u> fella!)

A few years later, Al wiggled his way into a squadron equipped with the brand new F-8, Crusaders—a really great flying machine for its era! On deployment to Atsugi, Japan, the Commanding Officer of the Squadron picked up on the "Animal" routine, and started calling Al "His Perpetual On Liberty, Liberty Risk!"

Since the CO was all over him'—like ALL of his past Commanding Officers had been—he thought it would be a good idea if he "cleaned up his act . . . . just a little."

Accordingly, when he went back to the States, the Blue Angels were just beginning to start flying F-11F Tigers. Normally, whoever was trying out for The Blues would get checked out in the Tiger, and they would get checked out at NAS Beeville, in The Animal's Squadron. The Animal was assigned to be the Instructor.

So, in rolled Fred "Beans" Craig (USMC).

(Break/Break: The Animal told me to be sure to say, "Oh . . . . how that man can FART!)

Fred had been slated to be the Solo Pilot for the Blue Angels, and The Animal was to check him out as a Solo Pilot. (Note: The F-11 had "about" two (2) minutes of fuel because the fuel was (theoretically) trapped in a little container while the jet was inverted.) When "The Animal" was with his Instructor Under Training, the Animal would roll inverted shortly after Take Off, and climb out, inverted, with the IUT on his wing. One day he was really "into it," and rolled over at about 12,000 feet and climbed at about 250 knots. Passing about 17,000 feet . . . . EVERYTHING WENT QUIET.

Oops . . . . He started slowing down. Hmmm . . . . The Animal had "Flamed (himself) Out!"

With more than a bit of "pucker factor," he went through the Re-Light procedures. Pause. Pause . . . . and the boooorrr sound indicated that the engine was spooling up, and everything was coming back on-line—albeit slowly. He never said a word to his wingman, and as the engine spooled up, he gave his Wingman the nod for a "power up" signal, and continued on the mission.

It was supposed to be an ACM (Air Combat Maneuvering) sortie, but I think that he said, ("I don't recall that I did any more than 30 degrees angle of bank, and 2G's.) Hmmm, but it was also said that his Plane Captain had to use a putty knife to pry him off the ejection seat . . . .

Well, as you might guess, there are many, many more Sea (and other kinds of) stories about "The Animal, and, believe it or not, just about ALL of them are quite likely to be <u>TRUE</u>!

All of the folks who know him well realize that he is definitely a "One of a Kind" kinda guy!

Chapter 3

(Dragon)

Dragon is a close and very long duration friend of mine. He has done a "somewhat reasonable" job of keeping me out of trouble for MANY years, and I have done all I could do to reciprocate.

After playing football at the University of North Carolina, Randy thought it would be a "Manly" idea to join the Marine Corps, so he signed up. Like every other "potential" Marine Officer, Randy was assigned to The Basic School (AKA: TBS), located at Marine Corps Base (MCB) Quantico, Virginia. TBS is the venue that teaches, polishes, and hones successful Second Lieutenants, so as to become Leaders of Marines. A grueling six months are spent there learning, doing, and comprehending what being a Leader of Marines is all about. It is Marine Corps policy that ALL Officers are to be trained to be Infantrymen, so as to successfully lead at any time, in any clime, anywhere. That is where the rubber hits the road! The reason for that is very simple: If, a pilot, for instance, flying over a Marine Infantry unit, in a situation which has "Troops In Contact," and does NOT clearly understand what the Marines on the ground are doing and experiencing, he can't fully understand what the proper response can or should be (i.e. What degree of fire power; what type of weapon; how long his aircraft can loiter; how accurate the response has to be; etc.). In order to do that, the "Ground Pounder" folks must know what they want him to do, need to do, and why. Most of the time it's pretty straight-forward for experienced Marines, so that is why the Lieutenants are taught and trained—over and over—to "Always get it right the first time!"

Nearing the end of his training at The Basic School (TBS), Randy and his buddies had some free time, and had a beer or two, and decided to blow off some steam, so a few of them drove up to Washington, DC to take time off for some R&R (Rest and Reaction.)

After consuming some malt beverages, they decided to go over to the traveling circus, which they had noticed nearby. One of the first things that caught their collective eyes was the rather large crowd at the end of the midway. Upon investigation, they discovered an iron barred cage there, so they sauntered over to have a closer look. To their surprise, they found a little female Orangutan sitting in the big cage, peeling and eating a banana. She didn't appear to them to be very big, dangerous, or even the least bit agitated. The "Barker" immediately saw the fresh "high-and-tight" haircuts of the Marines, and asked, "Do any of you Marines want to try to wrestle my little ole orangutan? (Note: He knew they were Marines by their VERY short haircuts.) "Just give me five dollars, American, Marine, and, IF YOU CAN HACK IT by staying in the cage with her for 5 (five)-minutes—only 5 minutes! IF you can hack it, for 5 minutes, I will give anyone who can stay in there that long . . . $50 DOLLARS, American!

His pals were saying, "$50 dollars for just being in there? That's a piece of cake. You can DO it Randy!

Then, Lieutenant Brinkley said, "SURE! I CAN do it!"

As he entered the cage, the orangutan took a quick look at him, and then went back to eating her banana, looking at Randy just every once in a while. Randy's first thought was, "This is going to be a piece of cake. I wonder how much beer I can buy with that $50.00?"

The little ape looked docile enough: About 50 or 60 pounds (max) . . . Skinny arms . . . Reddish hair . . . Seemingly not interested in anything other than her banana. About that time, the Barker said something to the ape, and then "SMILED" at Randy. The ape dropped her banana, and headed for Randy, dragging her knuckles all the way. The crowd seemed to be rooting for the monkey! That was Randy's first clue. He began to have second thoughts, but he looked back at his buddies and gave them a big smile and a Thumbs Up, and then he said, "I'm goanna wrestle him!" (Well . . . . actually . . . . he was a "SHE.")

As she "clinched up" (just like in a choreographed televised wrestling match), Randy deftly spun around, got behind her back, and put her into a Full Nelson. She didn't seem to care very much, so he turned back to his buddies, and gave them a big grin. They were yelling and clapping. He was feeling pretty good about the whole thing, however things were about to happen which would change his state of mind considerably! While he was grinning to his buddies, the orangutan slowly slipped her left arm out of his Full Nelson (which, at this point, became a HALF Nelson).

You would think her arm was lubricated! She then reached up and grabbed a bar on the roof of the cage, and proceeded to perform a left-handed, one armed pull-up, with our hero (at about 220 pounds) now hanging on for dear life. Well, as you might have already inferred, the situation quickly went down-hill from there.

The orangutan wiggled around a bit, got entirely out of the other half of the "Nelson," and then slowly grabbed him by the scruff of his neck, and <u>threw</u> him across the cage, crashing him into the bars, about a foot off the ground . . . . (I am not making this up, folks! Well, not much . . . .) He slumped to the ground like a lumpy, beat-up, piece of protoplasm.

She walked over to beat him up some more, and then did a "stomp dance" on his face. His "buddies" were "trying" to help by wishing and yelling, (if that counts in that league), but, at the end, it was very obvious that she had beat him up pretty well.

Hmm. It would appear that she "may" have done something like this before . . . .

Well, she backed off, stared at him for a minute or two, and then went back to her banana for a few more bites, all the while dragging her knuckles. When Randy got out of the cage, a few people were smiling and/or giggling at him, the Barker was smiling, but Randy's buddies were not laughing. NO!—They were ROARING so hard and so loud that they couldn't even stand up or catch their breath!! Needless to say, they decided that it was probably a good time to drive back to The Basic School in Quantico.

At breakfast the next morning, our "hero" went down to the Officers' Mess, through the cafeteria-style breakfast line, and got his breakfast. He wasn't very hungry because his face hurt (He had <u>not</u> forgotten that the orangutan had done a "tap dance" on his face). As he looked for a place to sit, he noticed a fellow Marine Officer who looked like he had been in a serious car wreck . . . . so he sat down across the table from him, and said, "Geez! What happened to you? Were you in a car wreck?

"Nah," said Randy's breakfast buddy, "I just made the mistake of trying to wrestle a little, scrawny, female orangutan, and, well . . . . it didn't work out the way I thought it would . . . . So, what happened to you?

Our hero quickly thought, and replied, "Me? Oh, I just fell down a flight of stairs."

(Author's insert: Yeah, <u>SURE</u>!)

After spending a year in Viet Nam, as a "Weed Wiggler," "Grunt," "Ground Pounder," Infantry Officer (your choice) . . . . Lieutenant Brinkley decided that being a Grunt was a "bit" more than . . . . ahh . . . . "<u>sporty</u>" than he had expected during his "formative" year in Viet Nam. In addition, he had clearly decided that BIG guys make really good targets! Accordingly, after spending a year in Viet Nam, as a "Weed Wiggler," he decided to see if he could be a "Zoomie" (Aviator).

When he got back to the States, he began to ask a lot of questions. It sounded pretty cool, and he had already determined that he probably wouldn't have to hike for 20 miles with a 100 pound pack any more. Well, while he was back to the Basic School (as an Instructor), someone had told him that Marine Aviators sleep in air-conditioned BOQs (Bachelor Officers' Quarters) with running hot and cold water, air conditioning, and three square (hot) meals a day, made by someone else, for you every day! When he asked several of them, Off-Stage, they said, "Yeah. Sure." He also remembered from his Grunt days how "cool" it was to call in an A-4 or an F-4 loaded with wall-to-wall NAPALM to generate lots of enemy "attention."

When the USAF-trained Marines got to their USMC "Gun Squadrons," they were a bit behind their Navy Trained pals (the Air Force trained folks did not get Air to Air Gunnery, Air Combat Maneuvering, and Carrier Landings Qualification.) However, after a year back with the Corps, everything evened out.

Randy was assigned to an F-4 Phantom Training Squadron (VMFAT-101) at Marine Corps Air Station, Cherry Point, North Carolina. He was thrilled. (Among other things, he had grown up in North Carolina, and had attended—and played college football at North Carolina University.)

He was anxious to fly the F-4 . . . . a manly BEAST of the USMC/USN/USAF fighter communities back in those days, not too long ago! Randy soon met a Major by the name of Jack Hammond (Call Sign: "Snapper" . . . and for a good reason!).

There was a RIO (Radar Intercept Operator AKA the "GIB," (Guy In Back) assigned to be Randy's Instructor, and he "briefed" Randy by discussing what they had done (just as they had briefed it while on the ground), and emphasizing the differences between Sub-Sonic and Super-Sonic flight. Then, when he was finished with his spiel, he asked if Randy had any questions. Well, Randy immediately asked, "Can we go for Mach 2? We should have a lot of gas left!"

Well, it just so happened that the RIO had never gone Mach 2, himself . . . . so he said, "Why NOT. Let's GO for it!" The RIO was still talking as Randy lit the Burners again, this time heading South. In short order, they passed Mach 1, and pressed on. In a "New York minute they hit Mach 2. All they could say was WOW! With their hearts still beating hard, they slowly throttled back, caught their breath, and aimed the pointy-end toward Cherry Point, came into and hit the Break, and calmly landed.

As they were parking the jet, Major Jack Hammond (the Squadron Maintenance Officer) . . . . looked out his window to see how GREAT that newly painted F-4 looked . . . . but . . . . <u>OH</u> <u>NO</u>! They've stripped that great paint job off!

The Mini-Maj was infuriated! His face reddened, his screaming volume was pegged, and he wanted to know how this could <u>ever</u> happen! He crashed out the door, with fire in his eyes, with kick-ass on his mind!

Our ground troops were just now noticing the damage themselves, and, OH, MY! The Mini-Maj is already huffing over to TAN their HIDES! As the Mini-Maj slipped under the jet's Radom to check for damage on the other side, Captain Brinkley took a hard left turn, and smartly whisked himself away from the jet, and departed the Flight Line, the Squadron, then the Air Station, as well as the STATE, if he thought he could get away with it!

After that "event," the Mini-Major' immediately took time off for R&R, and Randy flew the last two sorties that he needed to satisfy the requirements to successfully pass through the entire syllabus.

Having completed that, he hastily jumped into his car, which was already packed and toped-off with gas, and headed due south. He reported that he could not help himself from constantly checking his rear-view mirror to see if a Marine Major was trying to catch him for about the first 100 miles!

Now, you may not believe this, but those two guys have been the "best of friends" now for about the high side of twenty years.

Go figure . . . .

Chapter 4

(Easy)

USN

(Former Top Gun Instructor)

It has been said that a good Fighter Pilot is a paranoid-narcissist. They think everyone is trying to kill them, yet, they also think that everyone loves them.

Accordingly, as you might have already discerned, the awarding of a Call Sign for Navy/Marine Corps (as well as "other service" aviators who have been assigned to fly with the Navy/Marine squadrons), is a singularly unique, yet formally unwritten process. After all, if the pilot believes that everyone loves him, and that he flies his flying machine with the skill of a seasoned veteran, then he might think that he ought to get a "way cool Sky God" kind of Call Sign. Well, sometimes that works out splendidly, yet there are times it does not. I was fortunate enough to get my "Easy" Call Sign because of the F-4 "fighting egg."

The F-4 Phantom II—in its day—was considered to be a "rocket ship with wings." It was powered by two (2) very powerful, brutish J-79 engines. Needless to say, it was an aircraft of tremendous power and acceleration. All of the Phantom pilots thought that these beautiful, <u>very</u> powerful, supersonic beasts had some really positive features; however, it could NOT turn in the horizontal plane with a Mig (read "Bad Guy") adversary. However, the F-4 <u>could</u> fight (in Air Combat Maneuvering) in, what was called, an "<u>energy fight</u>"—i.e. going straight up and strait down in the vertical plane. (Note: Visualize an egg, with its thicker/wider bottom.) OK, the F-4 is engaged by flying an attack pattern in a dogfight that fits the contour of a common chicken egg. In this manner, the F-4 could gain "angles" toward the aggressor's rear quarter, where the F-4s weaponry could be employed. The "Air To Mud Community" (Dive Bombers) said that this maneuvering worked so well that the F-4 was casually referred to as the "Fighting Egg."

But WAIT! The reader must know: <u>Why</u> would a Fighter capable of firing <u>B</u>eyond <u>V</u>isual <u>R</u>ange (BVR) missiles, using the radar guided "Sparrow" missile (A "Fox 1" shot) have that shot taken away, and be forced to engage up-close and personal in a "knife fight" to the death at all? Well, there are (at least) two (2) reasons:

- First, based upon personal experiences at Missile Shoot Exercises (i.e. Training to get ready for The Real

Thing), every Sparrow 1 fired was a perfect "Water Seeker!" It never missed the ocean, however, and it always missed the target that I was launching it toward!

- The second reason is that (even if the missile hit a target) that might not have been a good thing, either. It could be that the RIO (Radar Intercept Officer) could have accidently locked his RADAR on a "friendly" flying machine, and then tell the pilot he is cleared to shoot. (NOTE: Generally (under "normal" conditions) most F-4 crews liked to use the Ole—"One peek is worth a thousand sweeps" rule. (Translation: Get close enough to visually identify the aircraft which has been "locked-on" BEFORE you squeeze the trigger . . . . so as NOT to shoot down a "friendly" airplane.

Training for Viet Nam, and also manning the Hot Pad (at Naval Air Station Key West, Florida) so as to defend against potential Cuban-launched attacks (Yes! The Cubans—backed by the Russians—were flexing their muscles there for quite a while). Accordingly, Navy/USMC F-4 crews were ordered by Higher Headquarters to give up on firing Sparrow Missiles at BVR (Beyond Visual Range) in that arena. Visual identification was mandated/required—period.

Because of this hard requirement, a Section, which is a Navy/USMC tactical combat formation of two (2) fighters, flying in mutual support (called Loose Deuce formation), were required to identify and ascertain that the (Cuban?) bogies on their radars were actually "Bad Guys." These contingencies brought the F-4s "up close and personal" with the Cuban Migs, in what is often referred to as . . . . the "Knife Fight."

If many aircraft were involved, it would be called a "Fur Ball." (Note: The MIGS had a large tactical edge due to their much lighter wing-loading quotient, which gave them a better turning) capability). Accordingly, they flew in the horizontal (1st choice), while the F-4s worked in the vertical plane (because of their large thrust availability.)

Both the Marine Corps and the Navy flying F-4s used the semi-stripped down A-4 (Skyhawk) as an excellent training surrogate for a Mig. Those little, tight-turning "Scooters" were hard to fight and harder to see! To make it even harder, both the F-4 and the A-4 in our practice engagements are painted in flat gray, and armed with the heat-seeking AIM-9 Sidewinder series of missiles. The Sidewinder, when fired, is referred to as a Fox-2. (Note: When a Radar-Guided Sparrow is fired, it is referred to as a Fox-1.)

The general "gouge" for success is about one (1) mile at dead six o'clock (sorry, I should say "directly behind the target"), back in the Viet Nam Era, with a steady oral tone. That was the best/most successful cue for launching a successful AIM-9. Today—the AIM-9 is an "All Aspect" missile—meaning that it can even sense the heat from the FRONT of a jet engine (on some days!) All in all, it is an excellent air-to-air weapon. Once launched, it is a "fire and forget" weapon, so the person who pulled the trigger had better know for sure that he/she is tracking and firing on an enemy—not any of the "good guys!"

Now, the story of the day . . . . this is how a Call Sign was assigned to me:

Flying an F-4 in an ACM (Air Combat Maneuvering) training engagement with an A-4, I was trying to fight using the F-4 "Energy Fight"—which is dubbed as the "Fighting Egg." (Yup . . . . that's right!) By going straight up and straight down, with the goal of getting a (Sidewinder) tone on the A-4 (Read: MIG surrogate) who just couldn't get his nose pointed up at me, as I charged back down from my "High Yo-Yo" position into the fight. I was hoping that his horizontal turn would stand out against the ocean. At that moment, my RIO calmly called out, "Eeeeesy" very slowly on our intercom. I had gone into the vertical and was about 20,000 feet above the fight, and—as we would say at the bar and, there I was at 220 knots, flat on my back" . . . . so I pulled down hard, to go straight down-hill, selected full AB (After-Burners), and my 220 knot F-4 instantly became a super-sonic KILLER . . . . BUT there was one very big "gotcha"—pitching back into the fight in that manner raised the possibility of an overstress if the pilot didn't execute this maneuver smoothly and precisely. The F-4 had a "flying tail" (called a horizontal stabilizer) that could/would really "dig in" as the aircraft decelerated back through the speed of sound to slow down in order to pull some lead on an aggressor in order to get a good Sidewinder "tone."

Now, the F-4 Stabilator (i.e. Horizontal Flying Tail) was a really good thing (most of the time), but it had a very nasty habit of "digging in" when the Phantom transited back (down) through Mach 1.0 (the speed of sound) or more, when the jet had Gs on the airframe. This transition would lead to a very rapid increase of the "G" load on both crewmen, as well as the airframe IF the Pilot didn't go nice and easy on the stick during the transition/pull-out.

Now, in addition, the wonderful (sneaky "scoundrels") back at the MacDonald Aircraft Company had installed a reliable G-Meter in the wheel well of the airplane, which automatically kept a record of all the Gs which had been above the "Recommended/Ruled Limit." They needed this data so as to record all the Gs pulled over a baseline level so as to assure/know that the airframe had been overstressed. Over the years, this simple, quick check has, undoubtedly, saved many lives of many steely-eyed F-4 aircrews.

If significant Gs had been sustained, the F-4 "Turtle Back" (On the top of the fuselage) normally has to be opened and inspected. Guess who has the "OPPORTUNITY" to do this preparation? If my memory serves me correctly, it was the "lucky" gents who OVER-stressed the jet in the first place!

But, that's not the end of this story! OH, NO!

So, on one fateful day, screaming down-hill to fire a Fox-2 (Sidewinder) or two at that little ole A-4's six o'clock, my RIO realized that "my FANGS were out," and I really wanted to pull hard to win the engagement, but my RIO also realized that we were seconds away from a transonic overstress! Needless to say, he wanted to do with an overly aggressive pilot dumping a heavy paper workload on him, so he began a very calmly and soothing way said, "Easy—Easy—Easy!!"

Unfortunately, that transaction actually went out over the UHF (radio), instead of just on their internal intercom . . . . and . . . . so that was that for me!!

(Writer's Note: I never realized how easy "Easy" was!)

What's that? How do I know so much about this stuff? Well, I have had the (very) dubious distinction of having the "Honor" of UN-screwing each and every screw on both dorsal inspection plate doors of those 100+ (expletive deleted) screws on the "Turtle Back" of the F-4, so as to allow the Qualified Personnel to closely inspect every single inch of the two "Turtle Back" access door cavities. Once the detailed inspection was completed, and when all repairs are completed, the screws had to go back in—BUT—the Maintenance folks don't TRUST us nose-picking, College Boys to get the installation done <u>CORRECTLY</u> (and I don't blame them, because that will save my personal butt), so they do all of that by themselves.

Are you wondering to yourself how I have so much savvy about these screws? Well, I think I can probably share with you how I have acquired this valuable knowledge.

Well . . . . I was given several "special opportunities" to pull all the screws across the Turtle Back of the F-4 . . . . TWICE! (Guess I was slow learner!)

Chapter 5

"Whizzer"
USMC

It was March, 1980, and I had just completed the Basic Jet Syllabus in the Naval Air Training Command's VT-23 at Naval Air Station, Kingsville, Texas, and had been assigned as a student (AKA: Cone Head) to the Navy's Advanced Jet Training Squadron, VT-21, flying the TA-4 "Scooter." During my first week there, I was "recruited" (by Officers senior to me—which was just about everyone) to join the VT-21 Officers' Soft Ball Team. It just so happened, that the team's pitcher was the Squadron's Commending Officer. During my first game on this team I endeared myself to the "Skipper" by sliding safely into home plate, scoring the winning run, in the bottom of the last inning. That was the first time that the Skipper patted me on the back, and said, "Good job."

I felt pretty good about scoring the winning run, and looked forward to leveraging that accomplishment with my new Skipper (i.e. Commanding Officer) . . . . It is always good for the Skipper to know you, and like your act, during your first week in the squadron! (. . . . And, <u>no</u>, I was <u>not</u> a "<u>Brown Noser</u>"!).

Accordingly, I was looking forward to the next soft ball game, but, unbeknownst to me, my next meeting with the CO would have nothing to do with a softball, and everything to do with a Liberty incident.

During a "long weekend," three other VT-23 Student Naval Aviators and I decided to drive to Corpus Christi Beach, Texas, for a day's worth of R&R on the beach. We decided to take two cars, just as a precaution, since our cars were <u>not</u> "terribly reliable." A quick stop at an ABC Store filled the back seats of the cars nicely. Beer and tequila were the only choices, but there was plenty of each to carry us through to the next week or so. Somebody said that the beer makes the tequila "OK." Actually, I can't remember what we really said or did, but there was beer and tequila. Well, honestly, I can't remember <u>what</u> we said or <u>did</u>, but there was beer and vodka—no! Not Vodka—tequila! Yeah, that was it . . . .

On the way to the Beach, we made a pit stop at the Naval Air Station, Corpus Christi, to drop off one car. Once aboard NAS Corpus, we piled into my Datsun F-10, which seated four, with room for a BIG cooler. Unlike most beaches along the Gulf, you can drive your vehicle on the beach at

Corpus. After exhausting all the beer, and spending several hours catching some "rays," (not to mention a pretty good "buzz,") we headed back to NAS Corpus to retrieve (Ah . . . . actually, <u>find</u>) the car that we dropped off there. Our journey (looking for that vehicle), ultimately included an inadvertent detour through the NAS Corpus Officers' Base Housing. It was during the trip through "Officers' Row that I suddenly experienced the need to "relieve" myself . . . . if you know what I mean! While I was almost finished with my business, I heard, then saw, the folks who lived in that house . . . . then saw the folks who lived in that house and they were right where I was taking a whizz . . . . and their kids were there, too! The kids were giggling and pointing and laughing at me. Well, that's when I said all the things that I never should have said . . . .

I can't remember, but I was told that I orally fired back to them, with both barrels, and gave the parents/kids a really "bad show" regarding some raunchy words that I spewed. The next day, I was thinking that they may be residing in base housing . . . . in very close proximity to/or actually <u>IN</u> "Admirals' Row. Hmm. I just "might" be in in DEEP—"fecal material!" That ray of sobriety was akin to a good, old fashioned, "punch in the face!"

For a short time I tried to convince myself that I was hallucinating, but my buddies said, "Nah, that's what you said, all right!" One of the others chimed in with, "Yeah! Nice move, Bowles!"

Well, the "Fun Meter" was then "pegged," but not on the "positive" side. The following day I was flying "S-Patterns" in a Flight Simulator, the Instructor) told me that he had just been handed a note which said that I (Rick) needed to "Report to the Squadron Senior Marine as soon as I completed my simulator event.

Oh NO! This is <u>NOT</u> a "good" thing!

Needless to say, my control of the simulated airplane that I was flying left, ah . . . "something to be desired."

It immediately came to me that the previously discussed "Prop Puke" had methodically done his "homework." He likely surmised that my "high and tight" haircut, and my not-so-gracious, and, ah, UN-gentlemanly "encounter" with him, was probably indicative that the perpetrator was a dumbass Marine Student Naval Aviator. So, he simply ran the car's license plate number (via the Training Command's listings of all the cars registered on all Bases), took one short, walk down the hall of the NATC (<u>N</u>aval <u>A</u>viation <u>T</u>raining <u>C</u>ommand) Headquarters Building to "visit" the Senior Marine (a Hard Corps) no-nonsense Full Bird Colonel, who almost immediately kicked the "food chain," into high gear, and notified Rick's Squadron's Senior Marine to "FIX IT," and report back.

"The Hawg" is not a tiny guy. He's big, strong, and "Vee" shaped, works out every day, and has a deep, baritone voice that can make King Cong shiver! Ergo, you REALLY don't need to EVER rile this guy! Well, The Hawg got a loud verbal, ah let's just say, "rear end" chewing for "not supervising" his Marines in the Squadron properly, and that Rick really pissed the Colonel off.

Immediately after the simulation, Rick scooted over to his Squadron's spaces, went immediately to the office of Major Pete Hanner—who was the Squadron's Senior Marine, and the Squadron's Aircraft Maintenance Officer. Rick executed the appropriate "Three Raps" on the door facing, and, standing at Attention, properly reported "Lieutenant Dale reporting, as ordered, Sir!" Initially ignoring 1stLt Dale for a long time, the Major slowly and formally looked up from his paperwork, and blared, "GET IN HERE, Lieutenant." Rick quickly followed the order, and entered, then went back to the position of Attention, awaiting his fate. The following (one way) conversation was brief, and strikingly effective, as he slowly looked at Rick, and said: "So I heard from the Colonel that you got "Really Big" this week-end in Corpus. Could that possibly be TRUE?"

Rick: "Uh . . . . Yes, Sir!"

Major Hanner: "How long have you been in VT-21?"

Rick: "Uh, this is my second week, Sir."

Major Hanner: "Well, this is a long syllabus here in VT-21, and the next time I want to hear the CO say your name . . . . is at your "Winging!" <u>GOT THAT</u>?

Rick: "YES, SIR!"

Rick promptly performed an "About Face, and quickly left the Hawg's office, reached behind himself with both hands, to discover that he still had a BUTT, and headed up-stairs to the Ready Room, with his heart still pumping at an elevated rate! Once there, he approached the Squadron Duty Officer's desk, and intently looked out at the Flight Line, calming down.

Rick was not aware of anyone else in the ready room, but the Duty Officer and he. After just a few moments standing there, just looking out the window, the "Skipper" (Commanding Officer of the Squadron) appeared behind Rick's shoulder, with a big grin on his face.

Having been caught off-guard, all Rick could reply was, "Well, uh, HI, Skipper!"

Skipper Collins: "So, how are <u>YOU</u> doing today, Whizzer?"

Rick: "Uh . . . . Good, Sir! How are you?"

Skipper Collins: "I'm doing great . . . . . . <u>WHIZZER</u>!

Rick: "OK. See you, then, Sir."

Skipper Collins: "Yup . . . . See ya soon . . . . <u>WHIZZER</u>!

Well, the Commanding Officer, Commander J.C. Collins, and the Senior Marine, Major "Hawg" Hanner were big supporters for Rick for several months, and recommended that he remain in VT-21 as an Instructor Pilot. Although never done before (that we knew of), the request was sent to, and approved by Headquarters, Marine Corps. When he finished his tour, he was assigned to be the second Marine Corps' SERGRAD Instructor (AKA "Plow Back") Pilot in VT-21. On top of that, he was extended an extra six months over the normal 18 month tour so as to be able to compete to obtain orders to join the Marine Corps' first F/A-18 Hornet Squadron . . . and he <u>GOT</u> IT!

All of his is true.

I know.

I was THERE . . . . as the Exertive Officer of his Sister Squadron at Marine Corps Air Station, El Toro, California, flying brand-new F-18 Hornets!

In my book, he proved that he <u>was</u> as good as I hoped he would be!

Chapter 6

Stick

MIG Killer

USMC

You are about to read about a story which you are going to think was dreamed up in Hollywood. This is neither a fabrication nor a stretch of anyone's imagination. It is a <u>TRUE</u> story . . . . a FACTUAL report of what happened in the skies over Viet Nam on 12 August, 1972. It has come to be remembered as the ONLY, Never Having Been Done Before (or after, since that day), Air-To-Air kill of an enemy aircraft which has been credited to <u>THREE</u> (3) different United States Services!

Yes. You read that correctly:

Marine Corps

Navy, and

Air Force

Don't believe it? Then, read on!

Well, your Author was the Leader of the First Segment to get our (USMC) new "home" built and capable of flying tactical fighters & bombers (the Main Party) so that we all could kick some serious butt up North!

At the same time, there was also a Marine Fighter Pilot that had been assigned to the US Air Force—one who was concurrently, with the USAF units in Thailand at the same time (as The Marines). However, he was NOT in Nam Phong—a hot, barren, hot, dusty, hot "penal colony", (. . . did I say <u>HOT</u>?) as compared to the palatial U.S. Air Force accommodations further north, in Udorn!

After living in the desert for several months, the Marines in Nam Phong were finally allowed take to take their Liberty up to Udorn Air Force Base for "Rest and Relaxation." We were THRILLED to be able to be there.

"Stick" and Mike (An USAF "Weather Guesser") considered that they were "called up" by some crazy Air Force "Summer Help Program," but they were glad to accept abundance, well cared for F-4s, cold beer at the "Officers' Club," swimming pool, pretty nurses, etc. etc. and that they could almost "smell the gunpowder" (Stick's words).

Regardless of all of that, on 12 August, 1972, "Stick" was the Leader of a flight of four USAF Phantoms (F-4's) on a "Target Weather Observation" mission up in North Viet Nam. Their "formal" mission was to "Observe and Report" the conditions at the day's already targeted areas, so that the Strike Force would know what to except, regarding the weather, among other important things. Now, having said that, these guys were also hoping to find some Migs to, aha . . . . "eliminate"!

The POD (Plan Of the Day) was for a 0100 brief, a 0430 Launch, then hit the tanker (to fill up with jet fuel), and then press on to the Target Area. Under normal circumstances, they expected to make about three runs, each, dropping their bombs on the day's target, and then RTB (Return To Base). Headquarters would then make the decision to send or stand down the Main Strike Force, based upon what they (Stick and RIO) saw. On this particular day, the TOT (Time On Target) was slid back because of bad weather at Udorn. Accordingly, they had to wait until about 0700 to launch.

After Take-Off, they joined up with the airborne tanker, topped off their fuel supply, and headed North, coming into North Viet Nam, via Laos. They had potential targets to reconnoiter along the Red River, and on the North East railway. As they approached the Red River (60 to 70 miles west of Hanoi), they checked in with Red Crown (Air-Borne Control Center), and Red Crown advised the formation that there was going to be Mig activity out of Bullseye.

As they crossed the Red River, Red Crown called "Bandits airborne out of Bullseye, heading West, Angels 20!"

They acknowledged the data from Red Crown, and pressed on toward the target area. A few minutes later, Red Crown called "Bandits turning to a heading of 270. "Thud Ridge" was just disappearing under their noses as Red Crown called out that the bandits were disappearing under our noses, and are turning to 360, "at your six-o'clock, 30 miles, and attacking!

"Stick" slowed down, they punched off their centerline fuel tanks, pushed the power up, punched off their Center Line fuel tanks, and checked their "Fluid Four" formation. Everything looked good, and THE FIGHT WAS ON!

The "Good Guys" were at 15,000 feet as they began descending to pick up some speed for a possible engagement. As they continued South, Red Crown kept the position reports coming. The "shooters" were advised that there were two Mig-21s, at 18 miles. They searched for them with their own radars as they all went into afterburner to get rid of the notorious Phantom smoke trail behind them. They had a LOT of smash (read "speed") by this time, and figured that—IF they didn't spot them, they could just keep on going for home, because they wouldn't ever catch them if they passed beak to beak (AKA nose to nose).

As they continued South "at the speed of "stink," the calls from Red Crown indicated that the MIGs were drifting off to their (GOOD guys') port (left) side. The last call they got before picking them up visually was 120 at eight miles. They spotted the MIGS at four miles, as they were starting their stern conversion on the "Good Guys." They were supersonic, while the good guys were at .92 Mach. Stick reported, "I don't think they have acquired us, visually, but that they were only following the instructions of their GCI (Ground Control Information) Controller. The lead Mig-21 was silver, and his wingman was a mottled green camouflage (really pretty airplanes). The other two Migs were nowhere to be seen. So Stick reported Tally Ho on two, and they blew off their wing tanks, as the whole element began a slow port (left) turn, down inside of the Mig's turn. The Migs had begun a slow left turn, which they hoped would put them at "Stick's formation's" six o'clock. Dash 3 and 4 (the other element) went high, so as to be able to protect the "Good Guys, six o'clock. At about two (2) miles, the "good guys" got a solid radar lock on the lead Mig.

"Stick" didn't think that they saw them, as their maneuvers were not the least bit evasive. As they closed to a mile and a quarter, "Stick" fired a Sparrow (missile). The Sparrow came off his jet, and started leading out in front, toward a Mig. He was about 20-30 degrees off his tail, and something must have told him to look back just then.

He got the surprise of his life, because the Sparrow was about half-way to the targeted Mig when the BAD guy spotted it, and that big plume of smoke it trails, must have really gotten his adrenalin going! He reefed his jet right into Stick's section, and the missile went over the top of his jet. Stick couldn't tell if it was really as close as it looked, because the Sparrow did NOT detonate. They passed canopy-to-canopy, not more than a couple of hundred feet apart, he (the MIG) rolled toward Stick's six-o'clock, and dove out of sight. As he did that, Stick unloaded the jet, picked up some more knots, and locked onto his Wingman, who was still in his turn.

Stick had pretty much the same parameters for firing at the second Mig, and he launched another Sparrow. It came off the rail, smoked out in front of them, pulling lead on the Mig, and hit that Mig just forward of the vertical tail. The Mig snapped up, and rolled over into a spin as the vertical tail departed the aircraft. Stick said that he did not see any big fire-balls or plume of smoke, and as he (Stick) pulled up, he lost sight of him. The other (Good Guy) element came down, joined on them, and Stick called Red Crown to find out where the first Mig had gone. They told Stick that he was twelve miles away, and going strong for home, no doubt, in full After Burner!

The "Good Guys: hit the tanker, took gas, and Stick went just a little out of his way, on the way back to Udorn, and made a low, high speed pass for his Marine buddies at Nam Phong. (Author's note: While we were getting gas from "Fat Albert"—One of our KC-130 Tanker pilots told us that Stick did so many really fast rolls while going straight up over the Nam Phong runway, that the Marines on the ground thought "an Air Force "puke" (Not <u>MY</u> words, folks) had a "runway stick in that poor Air Force guy's Phantom!) BIG GRIN!

Stick & Company landed about 30 minutes later at Udorn after the "One Man Nam Pong Air Show," that day. I really wish I could have seen it, and subsequently pour beer on his head if he had landed at the Rose Garden!

A Quote: "They don't call him "Stick" because he's pretty, or that he has a lot of hair. They call him "<u>STICK</u>" because he can fly a fighter better than anyone else on the planet!" I completely agree with that assessment! The only down side of that for ME was that I didn't do it or say it FIRST!

Nice work and Semper Fi, Stick!

Chapter 7

"Boomer"
USMC

If you ever run into a guy who answers to "Boomer," I must tell you that there are precious few ways to be "awarded" that call sign!

What follows is one of the worst ways to get a Call Sign . . . short of crashing . . . and we already have guys out there with "Crash" on their name tags!

Boomer was an F-4 pilot, but had "graduated" to fly the brand-spanking new F/A-18 Strike/Fighter. He was a really GOOD F-4/F-18 pilot . . . however, one day while deployed to Marine Corps Air Station (MCAS), Yuma, Arizona he had the opportunity to fly an ACM (Air Combat Maneuvering) two (2) verses two (2) sortie on the TACTS Range (Tactical Aerial Combat Training System): a complex three-dimensional ground radar-based computer system which allows people on the ground to have interface with the airborne Fighters.

Note: The TACTS Range is QUITE exceptional, and is a super tool for honing the abilities of any level Fighter Pilot. When the pilots involved in the ACM sortie wish to see/ hear what happened, they can/should go over to the TACTS Range Control Room, and see exactly for themselves "Who Shot Whom, How, When, and to what degree," so as to learn (a lot) more about ACM (Air Combat Maneuvering).

During the mandatory Welcome Aboard Meeting at MCAS Yuma, ALL crewmen are REQUIRED to be briefed and—WARNED—that if ANYONE points their nose toward the schools and churches which are stretched along the North side of Interstate I-10 (the Northern boundary of the Air Combat Maneuvering Range), while they are headed North at a supersonic speed (i.e. causing a Sonic Boom . . . . which blows out windows and scares the MESS, out of the kids who live there . . . .), that pilot would immediately be physically removed from MCAS Yuma, and sent home to his own Squadron.

In the past, they have actually immediately flown "misbehaving" pilots (who broke any rule), back to their home base, sometimes in their own (MCAS Yuma) airplane!

Bob was what we call "A Natural" fighter pilot. He picked up just about everything in short order regarding flying a tactical jet fighter. He was also a "natural" leader, and his peers picked-up and used just about every "suggestion" he offered, especially regarding flying fighters. When his Squadron deployed to Marine Corps Air Station at Yuma, Arizona for Air-To-Ground and Air-To-Air training, they wanted to show the "world" how good they really were, especially with their BRAND NEW F/A-18s, by kicking some serious butt on the TACTS Range.

They began their ACM (Air Combat Maneuvering) training, working up the "Degree of Difficulty from 1 vs. 1, to 2 vs. 2, to 2 vs. UNKNOWN. Their initial "Aggressors" were USMC A-4s and USAF F-4s. The Training Schedule (as per the script) was based upon a continual increased "Degree of Difficulty" basis, so the Marines could be ready to "mix it up" with the USMC A-4s and F-4s, followed by some USAF F-4s, and/or F-15s as "Graduation" Exercises. All of these sorties were/ are conducted on the TACTS Range.

Bob's first two (2) hops (sorties) on the Range went quite well. He and his peers were on an almost vertical learning curve, and—most importantly—they were gaining confidence in their ability to fight . . . . and Win!

The Air Force "Brass" must have heard that the people they sent to Yuma were getting their butts kicked (like ya read about!), so they decided to try to level the playing field by sending their "Big Boys" (F-15 Eagles). The Marines were,

Ah . . . . "respectful" about it all, (but were giving each other "Hi 5's" back in their own Ready Rooms). However, all of the cards had not yet been dealt . . . . yet.

When the Eagles showed up, an aura of (supposed) invincibility surrounded them, as they strutted around like peacocks, talking loud, wearing ascots while the Marines decided to use the ole "Awe Shucks," and "Golly Gee" facade.

From the very beginning, the Marines (using their well-honed "Loose Deuce" tactics) surprised the F-15 drivers. Upon landing, some of the Air Force jocks simply refused to attend the De-Brief, and instead, they went to the bar. After the Marines concluded their own De-Briefs, they also went to the bar, and found all the USAF folks already there . . . . but, not for long.

The USAF folks simply walked out when the Marines came in. The Marines were laughing and joking, and anxious to talk to some of the F-15 drivers, so that both units could learn from the others.

Well, that wasn't very friendly of them, was it?

Naturally, the Marines thought that it was hilarious! The senior F-15 driver got all of his cohorts together, and laid down the law about getting beat up by "ancient" fighters. (Which, of course, was <u>TRUE</u>!).

The Air Force guys went back to "Stupid Studies" that night, and, as a group, polished all their tactics, moves, communications, mutual support, etc. It was "back to the basics" for them. When the sun rose, the USAF pilots were in the "Kick Ass and Take Names" mood, and they had their "Game Faces" on.

Well, as you might expect, the USAF took off with revenge in their minds. In the very first fight—a 2 verses 2—"Brother Knudson," after making only 3 (three) turns, slid into the rear quarter of an F-15, allowed his "fangs" to come out in expectation of a "kill," and forgot that he—TOO—had a rear quarter, when his Wing Man yelled out, "Break Port . . . . <u>NOW</u>!"

Bob immediately did a <u>HARD</u> Slice Turn down and in, toward the "back door" F-15. When the Eagle over-shot, Bob dove for the deck in a crisp, High G, slice turn, coupled with a well-done disengagement maneuver, un-loaded, selected full afterburner, and scooted North, clearing his 6-Oclock as he went at the speed of "stink!" (. . . . and that's <u>REALLY</u> FAST!)

<u>That </u>is when things went . . . . well . . . . "Other than GOOD.

Bob's Flight Leader was yelling, screaming, and bawling, "PULL UP! SLOW DOWN! TURN PORT . . . . JUST TURN!

"Why?" . . . . you might ask: "<u>WHY</u> did everyone go so spastic?

Well . . . . you might remember the warning which was rendered to you, earlier? You know—the one about schools and churches, and how supersonic flight in their proximity is a <u>REALLY BAD thing</u>, as well as an <u>ILLEGAL</u> thing to do.

Remember?

Well, to make a very long story a bit shorter, I can report what happened to the town which was "BOOMED."

It was a Sunday Morning, so the church was:

"Only" about half full,

"Only" 5 Stained Glass windows were blown in,

"Only" about 10 clear windows were blown in/out,

"Only" several houses facing Southwest had ALL their windows blown in/out,

"Only" half of the 4 gas pumps were functional.

(Well . . . . other than that Mrs. Lincoln, what did you think of the play?)

As he parked his jet, at MCAS Yuma, his RIO summed it all up perfectly, when he said, "We're <u>TOAST</u>!! Check your 2 O'clock!"

It turned out that his RIO was <u>not</u> mistaken . . . .

A crowd quickly gathered—<u>all</u> of whom had been specifically awaiting their arrival. The entourage was led by the Air Base Commander—a Marine Full Bird Colonel. The Colonel's greeting was terse: "Get your gear, and be back here in 10 minutes. You will be off my Base no later than 20 minutes from now. My people have been briefed of that schedule. Questions? Pause.

RIGHT! You <u>shouldn't</u> have any, so <u>GET OUT</u> of here!"

So, Bob became a bit of an inverse celebrity—like it or not. When he got back to his Squadron, his buddies were lurking for him, (along with the Squadron Commander) to hear what he had to say. They had heard about what happened, and so they decided—with the Skipper's blessing—upon the "PERFECT" Call Sign for him.

His Call Sign immediately became <u>Boomer</u>!

PS: Boomer is still flying as an American Airlines Captain. If you fly on American, be sure to look into the cockpit as you board, and see if you have him as your Captain. If it <u>is</u> him, just ask him if he intends to go supersonic on this flight, like he did over in Yuma when you broke all the windows?

He will say, "Who are you, and who in the world told you about that?"

Just grin and tell him that "Magic" sent me, and wants you to read his book!

Chapter 8

"Mad Dog"
USMC

Mad Dog and I met and became friends during our "internship" at The Basic School (TBS), in Quantico, Virginia, during the mid-60s. As far as I can recall, he showed up as just plain, ole "Dog." The background of how he got that nickname was not known by any of us, but, looking back, there was probably a really good story attached to the "Dog" moniker as well, however he still isn't talking!

Upon graduation from TBS, we were both ordered to report to Naval Air Station, Pensacola, Florida, to enter Pre-Flight and Flight Training. Upon our arrival, we were notified that there was a large backlog of Student Pilots. We were told that it might be as long as four to six months before we could begin our Flight Training.

Accordingly, we were assigned "very important and meaningful" (read "menial") jobs/tasks until our number was called for us to actually start our flight training. Speaking only for myself, this was how I learned the Navy/Marine Corps "Hurry up and Wait" paradigm.

Well, Mike was detailed to work in the Station Gym, initially telling us that he got a great job. We later discovered that he was put in charge of "jocks and socks."

On the other hand, I was assigned to be the Base's "Casualty Assistance Officer." Initially, I didn't know what that title <u>really</u> meant. I soon discovered that this poor guy (ME) had to go out to break the news to Moms, Dads, Kids, and Wives that their son, husband, dad, etc. will <u>NEVER</u> be coming home (except in a box).

Think . . . . just for a moment about that . . . . It is unequivocally the worst job in the Universe. I will spare you by <u>not</u> telling you about all the human reactions that occurred during those highly sensitive, electrical, tear—jerking, heart-breaking, depressing, devastating—BUT greatly needed sympathy visits—which are done by a Specific Service member (i.e. A Marine <u>Officer</u> "visits" a Marine casualty's family/next of kin.) I will tell you that every single one of those was a "gut wrenching" experience . . . . <u>EVERY</u> <u>TIME</u>. I had actually made as many as three different Condolence Calls in a single day <u>OFTEN</u> during the war in Viet Nam. (Aside: Don't let anybody EVER tell you that it was NOT a WAR!)

I normally had at least one visit <u>every</u> <u>day</u>, Monday through Sunday.

Our Naval Air Station, Pensacola Chaplin would always ride with me on every single call (as you might guess, religiously). So did the NAS (Naval Air Station) Pensacola Personal Affairs Officer, so as to inform the family what the Government will do, what they need to do themselves, and how and when they need to do it, etc., etc. Very rarely did the family hear a single word that the Personnel Officer said—poor guy. His main way of communicating with these poor people, was the Brochure, which he always left with them. It spelled out just about everything they could ever want/need to know as well as appropriate telephone numbers. Now, I knew from the start that this job was, most certainly, a <u>very</u> important job, but I just wasn't <u>UP</u> for being <u>DOWN</u> every single day! I wasn't sure what a "nervous" attack was, but I was pretty sure I had it on many occasions—whatever it was. So, on our next field visit, I (casually) told the Doc and the Chaplain my "symptoms," and asked them what I should do.

The Chaplain spoke first, and said, "Rich, I truly and fully understand. Please be assured that you are not the first person who ever felt overwhelmed and became very, very sad on this particular <u>Mission</u>. (<u>Mission</u>: He called it a "<u>Mission</u>," but he didn't mean a Military Mission). He continued . . . . Having been around you for the past two months, I have seen that you are a real "People Person," and it really bothers you that there is so much carnage associated with this Mission (Note, again, that he did not say "job.")

The car was completely quiet for about ten minutes, and then the Personnel Officer turned to the Chaplain, and said something like, "I must guess, that Rich has had his fill of this, Preacher. He has "lasted a lot longer than most of the others." Instantly, I was offended, and turned to reply to that statement, but the Chaplin quickly cut me off by showing me his palm, and said, "God go with you, Son. You will need him when you arrive in Viet Nam."

I was stunned.

All I could think to say was, "Well, Thanks, Chaplain, I don't plan on staying there for a long time . . . . It's just going to be some short visits, inland for me, so as to drop my bombs." Well, that was something that just came out. (Have you ever done that? Just askin' . . . .)

The Chaplin burst out laughing, but managed to quickly recover his decorum, and tried (hard) not to laugh out loud.

Then, they both laughed, knowingly.

The next day I was ordered to report back to the MAD (Marine Air Detachment). To my surprise, I was assigned to Mad Dog's previous job at the Gym!! He had been given a reprieve for some innocuous reason. How did he do that? After a week, I was dismissed from that job. (Hmmm . . . . I didn't screw anything up, but I knew better than to actually ASK WHY I was dismissed, because that might "inspire" someone to come up with a job like cleaning the toilets, or something worse."

By this time in my short Marine career, I was ushered back into the "Students' Pool," where I vegetated for another several months before I actually began my flight training. Accordingly, I became a Gym Rat again, and pumped my body up for the adventure that was soon to begin for me. The Dog and I (frankly) had too much time on our hands during that time frame. We hit the pavement almost every night, and got into trouble, ah . . . . let's just say, "only every once in a while."

We finally got to start the first segment of our training, there in Pensacola (Primary Training), flying T-34s, got our (traditional) ties cut off when we <u>lived</u> and <u>survived</u> that first solo flight . . . . and I still have MY TIE!

We were then shipped off to Naval Air Station' Meridian, located at Meridian, Mississippi. We were there to learn how to fly our first <u>jet</u> trainer: the T-2 (Buckeye). Because the Naval Air Training Command was being pushed HARD to deliver many more pilots to fight the war in Viet Nam, everyone was doing every-thing they could do, and then some. The Admiral ordered that the PTR (Pilot Training Rate) be accelerated as much as humanly possible. Accordingly, most academic classes were taught at night, while the other Instructors and Students flew during the day.

One night, MD and I sat in a Class Room for a mandatory instructional event, with about 30 other "Cone Heads"—as the Instructors called us jokingly—(I think), and we were getting bored (like you read about!). The Instructor's voice was Hum-Drum, and his mumbled, monosyllabic delivery was not understandable, and did I say terrible?

MD and I were trying real hard to listen to what the guy was saying, but the snoring from all the guys in front of us was droning out whatever he was saying. Yawns proliferated throughout the room, and the temperature seemed that it was always rising. In my mind, I was yelling, "Get to the point, man! Come ON!" Unfortunately, I truly believe that his main focus was that he didn't really HAVE a focus!

About that time, I saw a big, black spider on the floor. It then started up Mad Dog's desk leg. As the good buddy that I was, I gave MD a "psssst." No response. Then then I gave him a "A-hem." When he looked over . . . .

(Ah, HA! He had been sound asleep!) . . . . so I pointed to the spider, which was just arriving at the top of Dog's desk. As the spider started walking across the desk—like he OWNED the place—MD scarfed it up in his right hand, looked over at me, smiled, and threw that big ole (possible Black Widow) spider into his mouth! Well, he didn't get it all the way in, so the spider's legs were sticking out between his lips, and were just a-wigglin'!

Although I turned my eyes away, and tried <u>REAL</u> hard, to suppress my laugh, I must have made some sort of noise, because the Instructor asked me if I needed a glass of water. I coolly and very politely said, "No, Sir, but thank, you, Sir," and looked up at the dirty ceiling, while I was pinching my forearm so as not to laugh again. When I thought I was all right, I took a peek of Mad Dog, and what I saw just <u>cracked me up</u>! He still had the spider in his mouth, and all of the spider's eight legs were still sticking out between his lips, and were just a' wigglin' at about a mile a minute! He then closed the show, by doing a Chomp, Chomp, Chomp, and <u>swallowed</u> the spider!

I considered choking myself to keep from laughing out loud, but it didn't work. The Instructor asked me again if I had a problem, but I said, "No Sir, but I think I need to go to the Head (i.e. toilet), Sir.

He just said (I think in disgust), "Never mind! Class Dismissed."

Mad Dog and I roared with laughter all the way back to our BOQ (Bachelors Officer's Quarters) rooms.

When I saw him the next morning at breakfast, I asked him, "How was your aracnapod dinner last night?"

He replied, "It was wiggly . . . . all the way down!"

When we completed that particular block of training, we were—once again—sent off to another Navy Training Base. This time we found ourselves at Main Side, NAS Pensacola. We were there for Aerial Gunnery and Carrier Qualification (AKA—"Hitting the Boat!").

I found Air-To-Air Gunnery to be a BLAST! I think I must have been born with the ability to adroitly maneuver in 3-Dimentional space, and accept and control high-Gs, constantly changing so as to co-exist with my fellows (three other "Cone Heads" like me) in the Gunnery Pattern, with precious little room for error. I must admit that it gave me a good dose of adrenalin.

Ole Mad Dog did quite well in the Gun Pattern, as well.

We both thought it was pretty cool to be competing with our Classmates, but even better to be pushing each other to get better, and better, and better.

Next, we tackled the "Art" of landing on an Aircraft Carrier. After many, many, many, many practice hops (flights) learning how to "Fly The Ball" so as to "Catch a wire—preferably the #3 wire" (Which is referred to as the "Target" wire). After much practicing on land, we were told that we were ready to "Hit the Boat" for the first time.

Author's Note: Sailors just <u>HATE</u> it when anyone refers to any ship as a <u>boat</u> . . . . so, of course, we Marines would go out of our way to <u>ALWAYS</u> call it "The Boat!" It was great "intermural" jousting!

ASIDE: The Black Shoe Navy—the folks who run/"Sail" the ships—wear black shoes, while the Navy Aviators wear brown shoes. The "Black Shoes" get WAY out of control when someone/anyone refers their SHIP as a BOAT. They constantly insist that a SHIP <u>carries</u> BOATS—Got It? "Yeah. We get it. We simply refer to your vessel as a BOAT to ascertain that you are listening to what we are saying to you!" Well, our Boat/Ship was the USS Lexington, a "27-Charlie" that was left over from WWII . . . . it even had a <u>wooden</u> deck! In spite of her short-comings, we Cone-Heads thought she was big and beautiful.

When we launched to <u>really</u> go "Hit the Boat" for the first time, we all were raring to go and upbeat. As we slipped into a Holding Pattern, well above the ship, I looked down to see the Lexington . . . . I was taken aback. "Oh, wow . . . . We are going to land on THAT little boat?"

The next thing I knew, we were flying over Lady Lex, and, one by one, we pitched off to the Port (Left) side at the requisite (extended) interval . . . . and, then, thank-fully, She no longer looked so little!

OK, it is now time for the Landing Check List: Landing Gear-Down, Flaps-Down, Hook-Down (<u>Only when the LSO tells you to drop it</u>), Harness—Locked, Fuel State—Look at your fuel gauge.

(Note: LSO = <u>L</u>anding <u>S</u>ignals <u>O</u>fficer).

We all were allowed to have two (2) Touch and Goes. If we looked "OK" to the LSO, we were told to go "HOOK DOWN." I still remember almost everything that occurred during my first Hook Down Pass: I was 101% focused, and hit all of my "gouge" check points as I turned in, right on the money. When I rolled out in the groove, the LSO told me to "Call the Ball." I replied and pulled just a bit of power, dipped the nose just a bit, then went right back to the attitude that I had previously. I was about to add power when the LSO very smoothly called "PowErrrr," and when I got "in close" I got a quick call of "Left for Line Up," and BLAM! I was on the deck! Wow!! What an adrenalin <u>RUSH</u>!! (Aside: I think I will <u>always</u> remember my first "Trap!")

I am sure no one will believe this, BUT—no kidding—my first real Carrier Landing was scored by the LSO as an OK—3 Wire! <u>Really</u>? WOW! That means that it was a <u>PERFICT LANDING</u>! <u>WHAT A RUSH</u>!

When I was shot off the bow (the Cat Shot), I immediately thought: "This is amazing. It's a sea-going amusement park . . . . WOW!"

The Dog was doing his "thing" as well, and both of us were happy "campers" when we got back to NAS Pensacola! I suppose it doesn't HAVE to be said, but . . . . we went out on the town to celebrate that night.

I think that each of us "Tail Hookers" look back to those days, and remember them like they were yesterday.

Chapter 9

"The Bear"
(RIP)

(Bear's favorite saying: "<u>Fat guys can pull more G's</u>.")

There may have been duos which could possibly be considered to be <u>almost</u> as good as Lee T. Lassiter (The Bear) and John Cummings (Little John), however I certainly haven't come across any of them, as of yet. The Bear was just about as big as a real bear, and Little John was exactly the opposite. In practice ACM (<u>A</u>ir <u>C</u>ombat <u>M</u>aneuvering), if you were to find yourself in a "Fur Ball" ("Dog Fight") with those guys, your best tactical option would be to immediately go to Full After Burner, unload, and get yourself out of the way, or they will beat you up "LIKE YOU READ ABOUT!"

Now, I don't know, and no one that I know knows, of anyone else that could adroitly and smoothly maneuver and work the Radar in the F-4 the way those gents could. They could do things with the F-4 that (theoretically) could NOT be done—and, most of the time without even breaking a "sweat."

No matter how hard I worked (in the Manuals, in the gym, or in the air), I couldn't come close to The Bear in the ACM (Air Combat Maneuvering) arena . . . . unless, of course, if he just let me . . . . so I could actually learn something!). However, every time we got back on the deck, in the De-Briefing Room, the Big Guy would go over all of my "Goods," and then patiently de-brief my "Others" in great detail. He is the guy who really taught me how to fly the F-4 properly.

If someone asked me right now, I would say that The Bear was about 6 foot 4 and weighed in at around 230+ pounds (when he was dieting . . . . which was approximately never). The Bear's premise was that "fat guys can pull more Gs." We all would chuckle, but his "Fatness Works" position just didn't go along very well with the senior "BRASS." In fact, they didn't approve it much at ALL! The Bear just did what he knew how to do—Shoot down Migs/et.al.

Now, when The Bear was happy, he would hum. That's correct . . . hum. He hummed whenever he was happy, and that was almost all the time. If you were fishing with him, you could always hear the Hum. If he was flying, and he was doing good (which was almost always), you could even hear him humming when he keyed the microphone, just prior to transmitting. I always got my butt waxed when I flew 1vs1 ACM (<u>A</u>ir <u>C</u>ombat <u>M</u>aneuvering) with The Bear. I mean, we were in different <u>LEAGUES!</u> He was in the Majors, and I was still in Little League, in comparison (. . . . and so was everyone else, if they were "man enough" to admit it!)

Little John (the Bear's close friend and his favorite RIO) had it all figured out. When he was in a good mood, he would often humm his "Bear Songs," some of which were as long as he wanted them to be!

Little John can corroborate all of that, because <u>he had been sitting right behind the Bear for many years!</u>

I had been in VMFA-333 (The Shamrocks) for some time when The Bear checked in to become our Commanding Officer, and—needless to say—Little John Cummings joined us shortly thereafter. We liked to call them "The Dynamic Duo!" The "Dynamic Duo" made it a point to fly with every pilot and every RIO assigned to the Squadron—they were feeling-out what kind of "Sticks and Scopes" they now had under their wings. That was a <u>very</u> good plan. Everyone was thrilled to have these two great guys on board, leading the pack, and teaching us by their great example.

After being together for several months, the time came around for the Squadron to run the Semi-Annual PFT

(<u>P</u>hysical <u>F</u>itness <u>T</u>est). Of course, it was an "All Hands" event. The PFT consisted of three (3) events: 1) Pull Ups; 2) Sit-Ups; and 3) A three mile run (for time). The Troops knew the "drill. Most of them ran every day, so he didn't <u>have</u> to tell them. However, Bear added, WE <u>ARE</u> GONNA DO IT, and do it <u>RIGHT</u>!

Well, The Troops loved The Bear, too. They quietly referred to him as "The Gentle Bear.")

(I must say that they got it pretty close to reality!)

The Bear then said: "I will run so as to ensure that I finish "On Time." I will finish <u>exactly</u> on time. <u>YOU WILL BE IN FRONT of me—GOT IT?"</u>

<u>The Troops barked: SIR, YES, SIR!</u>

So, off we went. With about a mile to go, I slowed, and doubled back to see how the Boss was doing (. . . . The 3-mile run was not the Boss' "Cup of Tea").

He was looking OK, but he wasn't moving as fast as I thought he needed to be going, so I "diplomatically" suggested that he might want to pick-up the pace. The Boss gasped a bit, and said, "Nah. I'm <u>right</u> where I'm supposed to be"—pointing to his watch. At this point, he was pretty red in the face and breathing deeply, so I decided to run along with him. When we finished, we smiled a lot, drank a lot of water, messed around, and then wandered back to the Squadron area. We showered and got dressed into our "Charlie Uniforms" so as to be "presentable" for Happy Hour at the Officers' Club . . . . to "restore our electrolytes," after all that hard exercising . . . . of course.

While I was sitting at my desk, clearing out some business, The Bear—all cleaned up, but still sweating—slipped into my office, sat down, closed the door, and said, "Well ? . . . ."

We were both tired, so I chuckled, as I said, "Ahhh, Well <u>what</u> Boss?"

"Well, how do you think the PFT went?"

I said, "Well, I think it was OK, Boss . . . . Not GREAT, but its OK. We will get a lot better in no time"

He looked at the ceiling for a bit, and then said, "Slow Watch."

I said, "Sir?"

He said, "Slow watch. I picked the wrong watch from my drawer at my house, and accidently used it in the run, today.

I said, "Think it would have made a difference?"

"I don't know," he said, "but it runs a lot slower than my other watch . . . . The one I <u>intended</u> to wear for the PFT."

"Sir, I strongly suggest that you immediately "LOSE" that "slow moving" watch into the "Dipsty Dumpster."

"Harumpf . . . . Good plan! I knew I could count on you! See you at the O-Club . . . and he gave me a HEAVY slap on my back."

I said what I was supposed to say: "Yes, Sir!"

WHAT A GUY!!

Shortly after that, our Squadron, "Trip Tray," (VMFA-333) was selected to go to sea aboard the USS America, as a component of CAG 8 (<u>C</u>arrier <u>A</u>ir <u>G</u>roup 8). The squadron prepared for this new adventure with lots of gusto and vigor, and, in about nine (6) months later flew aboard their new home, the USS America, and immediately headed straight to the Western Pacific.

Unfortunately, I was not able to make that cruise with them. During our work-ups, our 9-month-old son was in a VERY serious medical condition, and needed a very complex, very difficult, open-heart operation. We took him to the best heart surgeon in the Country, and the operation was undertaken, yet the little fella didn't make it through the operation. My wife was totally devastated. I was the same, but I didn't dare to let her know how bad I was. I was in shock for quite a long time, yet I was doing my absolute best to focus away from our loss, and focus on "Flying the Ball," but it just wasn't working.

My great friend, Scotty Dudley (Note: We called each other "Pal" for years . . . . in fact, we still do!) was our Squadron's LSO (Landing Signals Officer), so he personally worked real hard to get me back up to speed (and gave me more practice "on the ball" sorties, that the other guys didn't get), but—no matter what he or I did, nothing turned the tide. I had slipped from being among the "good guys" to a guy who could not find his own butt . . . . even using both hands, let alone fly well enough to be flying an F-4 around the Ship—especially at night.

Scotty and Bear sat me down, and Bear took a deep breath and told me that I would not be going to sea with them. That really hurt, but I finally realized that if I DID sail with them, I would probably do something "other than good," and so, I took my beating like a man, and wished my close friends "Good Hunting."

Looking back, that was the day that I really grew up.

I had failed, and it REALLY hurt . . . .

Shortly, the USS America was sailing in the Gulf of Tonkin with VMFA-333 onboard. Not long after they got to the war they were hot to trot, and ready to give the "Bad Guys" a real BAD spanking. The Bear (with "Little John" in his back seat), and "Scotty" Dudley (The LSO—(Landing Signal Officer), who happened to be a guy with GREAT eyes, flying Dash-2, with "Diamond" Jim Brady flying in Scotty's' back seat.

Concurrently, I was in the proximity as well—with VMFA-323, based in Danang, South Viet Nam, with two other USMC F-4 Squadrons.

Author's Note: Just to remember, when this was actually happening, try to remember the many diplomatic-induced "Cease Fires" we had back then—I believe it was four (4)—ALL OF WHICH were schemes, cooked-up by the North Viet Nam leaders to get the USA to stop the bombing of North Viet Nam (so that they could relax, rearm, and transport a WHOLE LOT more bandages, bullets, bombs, and lots of other B.S. to South Viet Nam!).

NOTE: Such abject stupidity by our elected "Leaders" in Washington DC at that critical time in the war was considered by the American Military to be four (4) "egregious aiding and abetting the enemy" actions!

Unfortunately, none ever went to Court, and not even a slap on the Commies' wrists were applied for their crimes. MANY American lives were lost simply because our CONGRESS could not do their job.

One day, when the "smoke" cleared, and the "Bad Guys" had enough food, ammo, etc., the foreign ships pulled out of the BAD GUYS DIGS, and we were able to go back to doing what we were there to do!

(Note: The hairs on the back of my neck (still) automatically stand out at attention whenever I recall that unbelievable "Goat Rope"!)

BREAK! BREAK!

I'm sorry, but I have a really HARD time knowing that we did not make that place a big parking lot.

OK. Rant over . . .

Bear/Little John and Scotty/(Diamond) Jim were launched off the America to support the CAG-8 (Carrier Air Group 8) Air-To-Ground strike on many North Viet Nam targets, just south of Bulls Eye (Hanoi). As soon as they went "Feet Dry" (Over Land), everything in the whole area lit up like it was the 4th of July . . . . but they were NOT just fire crackers that they were throwing at the Strike Package! Tracers of high-caliber bullets were coming from everywhere, SAMs were being launched, and many MIG-17s and MIG-21s popped up on all the Good Guys. The "Good Guys" flying the US Fighters found themselves in a "Bogie Rich Environment"—right where a fighter pilot always wants to be—and their "fangs" came out as they swung into "Plan One." (Oh, by the way, a "<u>Bogie</u>" is a "Bad Guy".)

The situation was getting pretty hot, and the Bear started Humming (Remember, The Bear Hums when he's <u>HAPPY</u>!) Red Crown (Shipboard Radar Control) was spitting out multiple vectors toward the airborne Migs . . . . and our fighters found themselves in a "Bogey-Rich environment!" (Note: (MOST) fighter pilots <u>DREAM</u> to be in that situation!). Just prior to Red Crown calling "Merge Plot" (when Good Guy and Bad Guy come together on the RADAR screen), Scotty (a guy with <u>GREAT</u> eyes) spied a MIG-21 at their 11 O'clock, low, called it out, and the FIGHT WAS ON! Bear got his nose around to point at the MIG, while Scotty went to the vertical, cleared Bear's 6'Oclock, and looked for other Bad Boys, as The Bear got his "fangs" out.

The fight went on with the F-4s working in the vertical, and the Migs maneuvering in the horizontal plane. That was when Bear's Mig made a small mistake, and The Bear awarded him with an AIM-9 (HEAT-SEEKER) missile, and it "blew the

Mig into thousands of pieces!" They took that in stride, and kept looking for another Mig, checked their own fuel states (which were getting near "BINGO"—meaning time to leave with enough fuel so as to get home, plus a little to spare). The other Mig seemed <u>not</u> to be terribly anxious to get the same treatment that his Leader just got, so he "bugged out," likely running down in the weeds, headed for his home base.

Congratulations abounded! It was a great day for all . . . . except the little guy in the MIG. In addition, intelligence resources relayed to the ship that the famous Colonel Toom (the infamous "Good Guy Killer" who had <u>MANY,</u> MANY kills) did not return from his sortie, and no other MIGs were reported killed by anyone else that day. In addition, the intelligence "Spooks" reported that Col Toom never flew again after that day, so we know who shot whom.

Other "sensitive" Agencies also confirmed that Col. Toom never came home. Accordingly, common sense would clearly ascertain that The Bear and Little John had downed the best Mig driver that the NVA had!

Chapter 10

"Hound Dog"

The best Hound in the Naval Air Training Command!

An unusually well squared-away Navy Ensign applied three resounding raps on the frame of the Operations Officer's office door (meaning—ME), and loudly barked, "Ensign McClain requesting permission to speak to the Major, SIR! (Wow! Was I dreaming? Was this REALLY a "Squared Away" Ensign? I will have to <u>see</u> this!), so I loudly barked, "Enter!" The lad who stepped up to my desk obviously worked out, wore a "high & tight" haircut, displayed a squared-away uniform, a perfect "Gig Line," and well spit-shined shoes . . . . not that I was checking him out, of course. This gent was "NOT a "normal" Navy Ensign, so I said, "Good looking uniform, Ensign. What can I do for you today?"

He smartly barked, "Sir, I understand that the Major is a "fairly" good racquetball player, Sir", showing me all of his shiny teeth in a wide grin. I (cautiously) replied "Well, maybe so, but I'm still learning," (Trying hard to be humble . . . . I never was very good at that),” but I <u>have</u> won a “fair” amount of tournaments against some pretty good hombres), but there aren’t too many folks who are reasonably serious players around here.”

He straightened up even more and said, “That’s good, Sir! I’d like to give you a few pointers, *IF you’re UP to it, Sir!”*

All I could do was smile and shake my head. I didn’t bother to tell him that I had recently won several big Racquetball Tournaments, but I decided to show him, rather than tell him . . . . It would be “better” that way, but . . . . <u>I IMMEDIATELY liked this guy</u>! (So WHY is he in the NAVY? He walks, talks, and looks like a squared away <u>Marine</u>!) What’s the deal, here?

We played racquetball several times, and the first things that I noticed were that he was in great shape, and worked the court like “Mr. Hustle!”

Both of us had gotten “worthy” competition! It was good fun, and a tough “fight.” I was keeping up with this “youngster,” but both of us kept spewing sweat all over the floor, so we had to occasionally stop to clean up all of our sweaty face, legs, etc,) and the <u>floor</u>!

The next morning found me with the normal "Saturday morning Headache/Hangover" so I would always cut the grass. When I had just about finished the lawn, I saw a guy with a "High and Tight haircut pulling a <u>big</u> brand-new fishing boat . . . . and it was Hound Dog!

He tooted his horn a few times (thinking we didn't SEE him?) A crowd of my neighbors came over to "eye-ball" this ship that was about as big as a "steamer." WOW!

While I was conducting the "ritual fore to aft of someone else's new boat, my seven year-old son, Marc, was standing there, and he immediately and excitedly asked, "Can I go, too?"

But, before I could say anything, Hound Dog said, "SURE, Marc! You can come, too!"

Marc was thrilled.

Now, Marc had never fished from a boat before, so Hound Dog and I gave him some "Do's" and "Don'ts" on the way down to the fishin' hole. He seemed like he understood, and promised that he would comply.

Well, we somehow found the aquatic equivalent of the Main Lode at the second spot we tried. We were catching really nice-sized bass, with an occasional "whopper." Marc caught a couple, as well. As the wind picked up, we quietly let the anchor down, and the boat turned us around into the wind.

(Please remember that last sentence)

After a while, Marc was having a bit of trouble casting into the wind, lost his interest in fishing, and announced that he had to pee, and would just do it right off the bow of the boat. Like any good Dad, I started to jump up and say "NO!" but Hound Dog said, "No. No, Sir. Let the boy learn, Sir!" . . . . with a big smile on his face, and showing me a poncho in his hand. We immediately held it up, in front of us, and as soon as we got it up, we heard a torrent of loud "splats" hitting the poncho, and a loud "AHHHHHA" from Marc. Yup—he actually DID "piss into the wind!"

Poor Marc was really mad that he got soaked by his own pee, but he was even MADDER that we were laughing. Marc still remembers that day—but not fondly. However, he still thinks that Hound Dog is some kind of "cool god!"

When he asks me what Admiral Hound Dog is doing these days, I just say, "He's climbing up the "Food Chain," Marc . . . . but, there isn't much further for him to go!

Chapter 11

Mike "Mini" Mott
(RIP)

The "Mini Mott" was a very close friend of mine, as well as at LEAST a couple hundred other folks, as well. Mini always liked to say that when he was born, the folks "On High" asked him if he wanted to be: tall or smart. He said that he would prefer to be tall, smart, and well-hung. He was holding out for all three, but God said he would give him only one, and asked him which of the three he would desire?

Well, it took him a while, but he chose smart—real smart! My personal assessment was that Mini was an AMAZINGLY smart guy with a wonderful sense of humor.

When Kathy met Mini, she always thought he was the most handsome Marine on the Planet, so it turned out to be a perfect match. Everyone was happy.

I always told Mini (as well as anyone else who would listen) that he was the "biggest little guy" that I had ever known. In addition to that, he was just <u>brilliant</u>—especially when compared to all of us dumb jocks!

After flying with him a few times, I stopped taking notes on my "knee board." I did not do that simply because Mini could flawlessly <u>remember</u> every single little bit of information we received, or exactly what we did to whom, when we did it, and how it turned out. I told him that he ought to change his Call Sign to "R2-D2," but he said he wouldn't do that because it had too many syllables—TWICE as many as Min-ee. (Note: Brevity is PRECIOUS in any Air Combat Maneuvering engagement.) The guy could remember things that happened years ago, with crystal-clear accuracy. So, before one of you ask me, I must tell you right now that, "YES! Mini <u>was</u> a <u>LOT</u> smarter than I was, am now, or will EVER be!!" However, before you laugh at me, I am ready to "Make Book" that he was probably a whole lot smarter than any of us . . . . especially you, Puker!

Now, my goal in this Chapter is to give you an idea of the kind of guy that my little buddy really was. I hope I can communicate to you well enough to allow you to admire him, too, albeit posthumously.

Now, Mini was the smallest "Big Man," perhaps in the entire Marine Corps. Everything and anything he did, was done quickly, with great vigor and élan, so as to deliver a quality product, on time on <u>every</u> occasion. Not any bigger than a "minute," Mini could jump into a "hi-volume discussion" like he was <u>twice</u> his real size!! Before anyone could figure out the best way to "skin" the (proverbial) cat, Mini would have already done it in his head, and could be found already in-work on the incidentals!

"Doctor" Mott (. . . . as he liked to be called), and constantly called his close friends with the "Doctor" title as well), breezed through the Naval Air Training Command, got his NFO (<u>N</u>aval <u>F</u>light <u>O</u>fficer) Wings, trained at the F-4 RAG (<u>R</u>eplacement <u>A</u>ir <u>G</u>roup), and was then assigned to a tactical F-4 Squadron. He was later selected for Navy Test Pilot School, as an NFO (<u>N</u>aval <u>F</u>light <u>O</u>fficer), and then back to fighters again.

The years sped by, and we found ourselves serving together at MAWTS-1 (<u>M</u>arine <u>A</u>viation <u>W</u>eapons and <u>T</u>raining <u>S</u>quadron One), at Marine Corps Air Station, Yuma, Arizona. MAWTS-1's Charter was to train all USMC <u>W</u>eapons <u>T</u>actics <u>I</u>nstructors (WTIs), and, execute other "sensitive/classified assignments."

So as to comply with that was dubbed (in classic bureaucratic lingo) ADT&E ("<u>A</u>dvanced <u>D</u>evelopment <u>T</u>est and Evaluation"), led by "Mini" Mott. The ADT&E charter was to serve as a "USMC Think Tank" for Better, Faster, and Cheaper Marine Corps Aviation solutions, as well as the development of new and unique USMC war-fighting capabilities.

On one occasion, Mini asked me if I "wanted to do some REAL work. (Yes . . . that was a friendly "dig," because I was the XO (Executive Officer)—the dirty, rotten scoundrel who was "always giving him (and everybody else, of course), something to put in their "Gotta Do" box.)

It turned out that we (meaning MAWTS-1) had been "invited" to send a crew (Pilot and RIO—Radar Intercept Officer) to the Boeing plant in Saint Louis to participate in several (Classified, at that time) simulated F/A-18 missions in the Boeing simulators. We were invited regarding the introduction of the brand new (at that time) two-seater, down & dirty, Night Attack Hornet. Now, I could tell you everything that we did and said, but if I do, I will have to kill you, because a lot of that stuff is CLASSIFIED . . . . Some of it was/is WAY classified. I can, however, give you a completely UNCLASSIFIED version of some of the things that transpired.

Upon our Noon arrival, we met up with several of our USMC and USN buddies, and, like us, they were paired up for whatever we were going to be asked to do. After an entire day of briefings regarding what we were to do for the rest of the week, we took our GIBS (<u>G</u>uys <u>I</u>n the <u>B</u>ack <u>S</u>eat) for a demonstration ride regarding what the F-18 can really do . . . . in a simulator.

After a quick "spin" in the Simulator so that they could get a feel of what the Hornet can do, as well as where all the "Switches, Bells, and Whistles" are in the rear cockpit.

The morning of the next day was spent being briefed on the F/A-18 (for the former RIOs, BNs, & "others"), a quick yet detailed agenda for each event for each crew, as well as a few more "warm-ups" for the folks who wanted a bit more F/A-18 familiarization time.

The afternoon was for "Solo Hornet pilots only, so as to "warm up" the Hornet pilots [and what they didn't tell us—to determine each pilot's general capability]. I found out later that I did pretty well on my runs in the SIMs (simulators) that day (Note: My personal premise was that you can't crash and die in a simulator, so I wanted to try all my crazy, off-the-wall ideas <u>only</u> in a simulator!).

With that in mind, I bagged (shot down) three (3) "simulated" bad guy aggressors," got to the targets just a tick or two close to "On Time," got good hits on the assigned targets, and got home "alive" each time. Although it might look pretty good on paper, I was soaking wet when I climbed out of the Simulator! Those dog-gone simulators get more realistic every day! I think the guys on the console (who knew me well from my many other visits to their site) must have turned up the "gain" (degree of difficulty) on the simulator "just for me!" . . . . and I WILL remember that one, boys!)

Yup. Sure enough, those guys were really yuckin' it up and slapping their legs when they saw me get out of the SIM ALL WET! (Hmmm . . . . that reminds me—I never <u>DID</u> get back at those "Computer Geeks" who ran the Simulator for making me <u>sweat</u> like that!!)

That night, Mini and I put our "Winning Game Plan" together for our crewed-up sorties, and made sure we both knew what either of us would be doing at any given time in the Simulator. The plan was both simple and easily memorable.

The next morning—as a joke—we "briefed" in front of everyone who was there:

> "OK. Here's the Brief: Magic does the
> Pilot "stuff" and Mini does the RIO "stuff."
> "Questions?
> Nope!
> Good! Let's "walk!"

We saw a lot of eyebrows snap up when we pulled that one on them. We both were still grinning as we climbed into the Simulator . . . . To make a long story short, we did well . . . . and we did OK on the next days, too. We could tell that the Simulator guys were "turning up the degree-of-difficulty" a bit higher on every sortie. Good! Let's ring this Simulator out <u>now</u>, instead of later and have to spend a whole BUNCH of bucks to correct any shortfalls. As we worked through the week, the missions they assigned to us became sequentially more difficult, sortie by sortie.

By mid-week we felt that we were trying to fly and WIN at the PhD level! A couple of guys were very politely told that they could go home, because they were not doing terribly well.

On Friday morning we were to fly our "Graduation Exercise" sorties. They threw the "BOOK" at us! We were the first to run through the "Gauntlet." Let's just say that "It was more than just a "friendly" flight. This time it was "nose to the grindstone" time."

We got everything but the kitchen sink thrown at us, but we chose to fight as hard as we could! During this period of time, I think . . . that we "might have used a few nasty ole cuss words" while we were fighting back this Goliath of a digital fighter airplane (Have you ever had the opportunity to go up against an electronic device as invincible as the Hydra? Well, WE did! Wow!)

We both were soaking wet when we got out of the simulator. One of the Engineers came into the De-Briefing room, and told us that he "thinks" that we are now Super Heroes!

My internal-warning devices were blaring, but I didn't know why . . . . but we were cued in when we were told that there was a School Teachers' group touring the plant (Thank God, without any kids), and had been watching and listening to every single thing we did/said on the Boeing TV System while we were in the simulator. I could never have articulated my embarrassment at that particular moment. I think that we might have—No, I KNOW WE DID—let a few rather "nasty" words out, as we were fighting the very realistic giant computer we were up against.

The Boeing Engineer said, "Oh NO! They <u>loved</u> it, and they want to meet you guys!"

Awe . . . . Man! No way! Uh . . . Uh . . . We have a plane to catch!" . . . . "Mini, we can de-brief at the Airport. Let's hit the road, right NOW!" Then, as if by "magic," we ran right into that whole bunch of teachers who where still hanging around in the Video Room seats—sitting on our only way out! They had been watching and listening to all the things we had been saying and doing on a really BIG screen right in front of their "bleacher" seats!

Well, we tried to be polite, and only told one little prevarication . . . . we said that we were late, and had to run to catch our airplane . . . . Actually, this was really semi-almost-sorta true! We showed our teeth, waved, and hit the road for the Airport.

After retirement from the Marine Corps, all three of us (Mini, Randy Brinkley, and I) were working together, once again, working for NASA. Mini was a "Big Wig" at NASA Headquarters, Randy was the Manager of the International Space Station (ISS), and I was the ISS International Partners' Director.

Then, the three of us found each other again, working for Boeing on the West Coast about five years or so later . . . . all of us working closely together . . . . for about four more years, until Mini got a great promotion to be the President of Boeing Space in Houston . . . . and I was invited to join him a month later to swing into another "Snake Oil" job, this time as a Boeing Vice President in Houston.

When Mini and I visited the Johnson Space Center Director, George Abbey, the first thing he mumbled to us was, "Well, I thought I got rid of you guys!"

Yeah, RIGHT, George! (He had a GREAT BIG GRIN on his face!")

Mini beat me to the punch word when he quickly added, "Yup! We're here to spend some of your money, too, George!" Sure enough, George continued to be our good friend, and was (in his own style) looking out for us. However, George would never admit that he even liked any of us . . . . but he was our "God Father" who was ALWAYS checking up on us, so that he knew what we were doing (Or, perhaps, what we were REALLY doing!). Well, things had been going quite well, so Mini sauntered into my office one day, closed the door, sat down, and put his feet up on my desk (What the heck . . . it was actually HIS desk!), and—out of the blue—said, "Ya know, Magic, it's time we have another PARTY!"

I felt obligated to remind him that he was still paying for the damages from the LAST party he threw!

"Nah", he said, I paid that off a long time ago . . . . and THIS time I will be more careful of who I invite."

"OK!" As they say, "It's YOUR party!"

Then he asked, "What about your Son-in-Law? Is he still staying at your house? You know—the big football player? Think he could hack it?"

I said, "Well, I'll ask, but I am pretty sure he won't turn down a party invitation from ANYBODY serving BOOZE!

He cracked up, slapped his leg (like he always did when he was happy), and, walking toward the door with me, said, "This will be a good time to see how he handles himself with "our crowd." Right then I knew that this was going to be "One of THOSE kind of parties!"

When we arrived at the Mott "mansion" the house was already filling up quickly—and it was a very large house! Most of the attendees were Marine/Navy Astronauts and a few "groundlings NASA folks, and all their spouses . . . . a really good bunch of great folks . . . . aah, at the start of the night, at least! Most of the men went upstairs to the "Mini Pub." (Trust me—The Pub was NOT "MINI" sized at all! He had every kind of booze, beer, wine, or whatever you could possibly imagine, and that included RUSSIAN VODKA that we both had bought home on one of our many Moscow (International Space Station) business trips.)

Mike—my Son-In-Law—was awe-struck!

After just a few hours the Guys were:

*Slurring their words

*Talking very loudly

*Approximately SEVEN feet tall (in their OWN minds)

*Occasionally passing gas which could be detected across the room (by hearing, smelling, or bragging)

*Demonstrating how to shoot your watch with your right hand (as if in aerial combat)

*Urinating in his pool because all the "Heads" were constantly occupied by the <u>women</u>!

*Asking a total stranger, "Hey, did I ever tell you the one about . . . ."

*Telling "Mini" jokes, etc.,

As the hour drew late, Kathy (Mini's wife) asked me, "Where's Mini?"

Hmmm . . . .

Nobody knew.

So, everybody searched all over the house, up and down stairs, all around, outside, in the pool, but we found no

Mini . . . . Kathy was getting really nervous about the situation, when Ashley (their Daughter) screeched out loud, and began hysterically laughing while covering her (now red) cheeks with her hands. She had discovered her father!

He was in the downstairs Coat Closet, lying on his back, all covered up under a big pile of coats (worn to his house by his many friends) . . . . SOUND ASLEEP (Read: Passed Out!) and SNORING!

The next morning my Son-In-Law (who was staying at our house) came downstairs (with a very obvious major league hang-over), and said, "WOW! That was <u>GREAT</u> last night! It was just like a FRATERNITY PARTY, except everyone was <u>OLD</u>!)

I could NOT top that one!

I sure do miss my little buddy . . . .

MINI REALLY WAS TRULY

<u>A GREAT</u> <u>AMERICAN</u>!

Chapter 12

(Sonny)

Flight Surgeon/Fighter Pilot/Astronaut

US Navy

Rest In Peace

I have personally had the great pleasure and honor of being a friend of this GREAT guy, who was also known as "Sonny" to his many friends. Note: He got to be called "Sonny" when he was just a kid, so that rolled over to his Call Sign very nicely. Sonny was a brilliant guy . . . a Doctor, a Flight Surgeon, a Jet Pilot, an Athlete, an Astronaut, and an absolutely AMAZING PERSON who was loved by everyone with whom he ever came in contact. I personally believed that my very competent friend could do just about ANYTHING!

The Marine Corps Air Station, in Beaufort, South Carolina was where I first met Sonny. He was the Flight Surgeon for Marine Air Group 31, and I was assigned to one of the F-4 Gun Squadrons there. The first time I met Sonny, I was very impressed. The more I got to know him, the more I liked and admired him. He was just "THAT Kind of Guy!"

I quickly discovered that he could do many things other than Medicine. He was a Marathon Runner, Scratch Golfer, Basketball Player, Racquetball Player, Anon. I soon found that he was a "Natural" flying an airplane, such as a TA-4, where he flew with me, quite often. Although he had no formal training in ACM (Air Combat Maneuvering), I worked with him, and soon he became a pretty decent ACM pilot in only about 4 months (and those words, spoken by a Fighter Pilot, should be read as a REALLY great achievement). Speaking of Fighter Pilots, he absolutely did NOT have a singular drop of arrogance in his body.

After he had been on board for a while, he decided to get the aviators in better shape. He would sit down next to a Pilot or RIO in a Ready Room, and get to know him, so as to get an idea how healthy he might be. Well, he would get to know him in a "New York Minute, and ask, "What do you do—you know—for exercise?"

The responder would usually hem and haw around, and would then say something, like, "Well, I like to run."

"GREAT!" Sonny would say. "Let's run the "X" miles you normally run for, say, five bucks? You win and I will give you

103

five bucks, and if I win you can give ME 5 bucks. What do you say? At that point, almost every Jar Head would say, "Sure, but I don't want to hurt you" . . . . BAM! The trap had been SPRUNG! Sonny could run like a gazelle!

Sometimes he would "troll" to get folks to golf, row, swim, play racket ball, lift weights, and even walk so as to get them back in shape, and <u>KEEP</u> THEM THERE! All he was trying to do was get those guys off their duffs and exercise like they SHOULD be doing! Yes, Sir! The new Flight Doc was a pretty "slick" fella!

Several years later, Sonny was selected to become an Astronaut. It was his life-long desire. Randy Brinkley and I were already in place at the Johnson Space Center, by that time, so we were elated that our buddy, Sonny, was coming down to Houston to be with us again! Well, naturally, like always before, Sonny was a big hit at NASA. Within two years, he was selected to fly in Space, and about a year later flew a very successful Space Shuttle mission. Having done that, he became a very often requested Astronaut Speaker.

Several months later, Sonny was dispatched to give a speech at a Convention in Georgia. Sonny and three other Astronauts had planned to bag a few hours of flight time, and fly a pair of NASA T-38s from Houston to Brunswick, Georgia. However, when they checked the weather and the forecast for Georgia, it was not even close to good enough for a T-38. So, Sonny and the guys talked it over, and rather quickly decided to have Sonny press on, Solo, but on a big commercial flying machine. The other guys would just go flying in the in the opposite direction (West).

Sonny got a ride to Hobby Airport and jumped into a two turbo-propped engine commercial "Bug Smasher." He sat down on an aisle seat, and found himself sitting next to Senator John Tower (Texas). I must assume that those two "talkers"—such as they both were—enjoyed each other's conversations. As they were descending, and getting close to the Brunswick Airport, whoever was flying the aircraft descended rapidly, and then rolled into some sort of "wrapped-up" turn to the left (so as to line-up with the runway? . . . . or what?). It seemed to be that the pilots could not feather the right engine prop nor get the wings level, and the aircraft augured straight down onto a rural road.

It was quite ironic that both Senator Tower and Sonny were both in that airplane because they chose to fly commercial, rather than flying their own airplanes into such inclement weather.

At least two (2) Great Americans departed from our planet on that dreary day.

May God have mercy on their souls.

Chapter 13

W. C. (Wil) Trafton

"Benjo"

When I first met Wil, I got the idea that he was answering to a Call Sign referring to a "Water Closet" and you know what happens in a water closet, right? So, I didn't really <u>WANT</u> to know how the guy got his WC, Call Sign! (However, I was later informed that WC is actually "<u>W</u>ilber <u>C</u>."

In reality, Wil and I are good friends. He spent 20 years in the Navy, flying an assortment of Attack machines. We have worked together at NASA, and then on some really big/intricate jobs/situations . . . . such as launching (Boeing) satellites, when I was a Boeing guy—often working hand-in-hand to execute a perfect launch on Wil's very cool, one of a kind, Sea Launch platform, where Wil was the "Head Hocho."

For many years, I didn't bother Wil about his Call Sign, simply because I thought he was, maybe, sensitive about it.

Well, as I was pulling this book together, I decided to call Wil, and ask if he wanted to be cited in this book. He said, "Sure." (Note: He and his wife were driving across the Country, on I-10.) We gabbed a while on my nickel, and what follows is what I discovered.

One of my questions was, "What would your initials, W.C. be if spelled out . . . <u>Water Cooler</u>, or <u>Water Closet</u>, or what? That's when he broke in! (He must have been having a good time or was <u>really</u> BOARED), and quickly ascertained that "W.C." were the initials for Wilber C. I said, OK, so what does the "C" stand for? He repeated "Wilber C." <u>OK</u>? . . . .

Well, I didn't really need to know that, anyway, so we dropped that, and, moving along, I asked him to remind me what his Call Sign was. He answered without hesitation, equivocation, or mental evasion—"BENJO." I was quite surprised, and I even knew another "Benjo."

You see, while in the Marine Corps, I have spent MANY tours of duty in the Orient—including Japan. So, over there, they have precious few sanitary sewage piping. So I said, "Yeah, right. You're kidding me, right?"

"Nope," he said. "Benjo" is what it is."

Now, this is probably a good time to change gears, and give you a really quick over-view about Benjos and other forms of, ah . . . . "sewage" in some rural areas in the Orient.

You see, a Benjo is a toilet, not terribly unlike the commodes of America and Europe 50 years ago. The major difference lies in the destination of the commodes' contents. The big cities have facilities just like we Americans have, however, in some "other than metropolitan" areas they have, well . . . . ditches. That's probably all you need/want to know, other than, the one thing I know you are going to ask about—"What about the smell," right?

Well, it <u>STINKS</u>! What would you expect? In addition, in the summer time, it <u>REALLY</u> stinks<u>!</u>

OK. I think you probably understand by now, so let's go to the Officers' Club, wherein you could find some good American food and the omnipresent well-stocked, American style bar! Well, after they checked in at the BOQ, they headed for the O'Club Bar. Now, back in those days, the Marines always had GREAT O'Clubs, with good chow and really cold beer, so the Squids—WHOOPS—I meant to say Naval Aviators—Gomen—bellied up to the bar, had a lot of fun, and closed the bar down whenever the bar-keeper HAD to leave.

Wil, somehow, got separated from his pals, and (we think) tried to walk to his BOQ room, so as to "hit the rack." Somewhere along his path, he got off the sidewalk, tripped, and fell . . . . right into a <u>BENJO DITCH</u>—which, as you might surmise, was full of, ah . . . let's just say excrement . . . . of every type, kind, smell, and/or color. Eyuk!

Well, THAT sobered him up immediately! He spat out benjo ditch Ahhh . . . . Ah . . . . other stuff that sorta looked like "water," and proceeded to spout a rather colorful assortment of curses. As he was pulling himself together, trying to calm down, he realized that: 1) He was suddenly quite cold, and 2) A Marine MP (<u>M</u>ilitary <u>P</u>olice) pick-up truck pulled up—lights flashing—and asked him "If he was having any trouble . . . ."

(Aside: What could you <u>possibly</u> say to the MP that he might understand as the truth? I was swimming laps? A midnight swim? Someone pushed me in?)

Well, he was lucky to be able to say, "Well, no. Not really, but I could really like to hitch a ride from you to the BOQ."

(Another aside: Can you imagine how HARD it must have been for that young Marine <u>NOT</u> to crack up laughing at this soaking wet Naval Officer who fell into the benjo ditch?)

Well, the MP thought it would be wise if he took him to the BOQ (<u>B</u>achelor <u>O</u>fficer <u>Q</u>uarters), but asked him very politely if he could ride in the back, in the truck's bed, and dutifully added, "Sir!" (Note: That Marine was a <u>really</u> GOOD GUY, and went out of his way to take good care of this Naval Officer, who just needed a little help.)

Wil spent a long time in the shower. He then washed his flight suit and skivvies, and threw them in to the drier. By morning, his "Zoom Bag" was dry, and didn't have (too much of) the fragrance of a benjo ditch.

When he met his buddies for breakfast, one immediately asked him, "Where did <u>YOU</u> go last night? Wil very calmly replied, "Aw, I wasn't feeling all that great, so I slipped back to the rack to get some sleep . . ."

And now yet another Naval Aviator could now be awarded the official Call Sign of "Benjo."

I can't imagine how many guys called "Benjo" are <u>REALLY</u> are out there, especially counting all the other Aviators who fell in, and managed to get cleaned up before anyone else saw or smelled them!

Chapter 14

"Puker"

Real Name Deleted by Request

When this writer served at MAWTS-1 (<u>M</u>arine <u>A</u>viation <u>W</u>eapons and <u>T</u>actics <u>S</u>quadron One) at MCAS (<u>M</u>arine <u>C</u>orps <u>A</u>ir <u>S</u>tation) in Yuma, Arizona, he was shuffled back and forth between the <u>E</u>xecutive <u>O</u>fficer (XO) job, and the <u>A</u>viation <u>S</u>afety <u>O</u>fficer (ASO) job. During one of the Bi-Annual WTI (<u>W</u>eapons and <u>T</u>actics <u>I</u>nstructor) training events, I sat down with the two augmentation Safety Officers, in my Office immediately upon their arrival. One was from a fixed-wing squadron, and the other from a rotary-wing squadron.

After having been given their specific orders regarding the six week's WTI Course, I informed them that strict and special emphasis MUST be constantly dedicated, and in the forefront every day/night during the entire course, ... <u>ESPECIALLY</u> during the airborne portion of the Course. I thought that they absorbed the orientation well, especially regarding the part about their specific duties to ENSURE that we had <u>NO MISHAPS</u> during the WTI training evolution. They took many notes, and seemed to be "up to the job," but both seemed a bit nervous about the titanic size of responsibility we had just assigned to them. (I didn't bother to tell them that I would also be working all Safety items, myself, so as to ensure that we had <u>NO</u> "Adverse Occurrences.")

After that, I tried to make them both a bit more comfortable regarding their duties, by asking them to tell me what their personal "Call Signs" were. The Fixed-Wing guy said his Call Sign was "Tweet," since he always seemed to be quite cheerful most all the time. As I was writing it down (so that I wouldn't forget), I asked the Rotary-wing guy what his Call Sign was. He—rather sheepishly—said that his Call Sign was "Puker." (Yes. That is right—PUKER!)

All I could say, was, "Ahhh, really? Puker, Huh?" I was looking away and pinching my ear lobe—HARD—so as <u>not</u> to laugh out loud . . . . but I couldn't help it, so I just said, "How in the world did you get <u>THAT</u> one? What did you <u>DO</u>?"

Without any hesitation, whatsoever, he told me his story . . . .

Two years prior to coming to MAWTS-1, he was stationed at MCAS New River (which is located just South of MCAS Cherry Point, North Carolina), a Helicopter MCAS (<u>M</u>arine

Corps Aviation Station). The Commandant of the Marine Corps had chosen to visit MCAS New River (a protocol/ inspection visit) while our "hero" was stationed there, and who was also selected to be a Platoon Leader (one of four) for the Parade for the Commandant.

The Marines, of course, were fastidiously practicing twice-a-day for the obligatory Parade. The weather was very hot and even more humid (MCAS New River is surrounded by water on three sides). The Parade "Participants" sweated through their uniforms after only a few minutes after starting their practice . . . . and, as you might guess, there were many practices.

At the same time, the newly hired Officers' Club Manager was pondering how to prepare and execute the customary Reception for the Commandant. He said that he had been told that the Officers had gotten rather rowdy in the past, when being offered free cold beer. He personally thought white wine would precipitate the same response, and hard liquor was completely out of the question. He, himself, personally decided that very few of these "animalistic" Marine Corps pilots would like red wine, so that was what he unilaterally decided to give to them (thinking that his idea would be a GREAT way to keep them from getting drunk, while in the presence of the Commandant.)

It would appear (to me) that he was trying to take the "EASY" way out.

(Opinion follows: Bad move. <u>REALLY</u> BAD move.)

On the day of the Commandant's visit, it was a very <u>hot</u> and <u>humid </u>day (as predicted), with little or no wind. As the Troops marched onto the Parade Deck, they were already soaking wet by the time they halted in their formations. An hour and a half later, after all the speeches, parading of all the Squadrons' Colors and the American Flag, and a few formal speeches, The Commandant requested the presence of all the Officers and their Ladies to join he and his wife at the Officers' Club. (An audible sigh could be heard, almost across the Parade Deck!)

EVERYONE was soaking wet, and on the look-out for something (anything!) cold to drink, only to discover that Red Wine was the only alcoholic beverage available.

As you might guess, all the Marine Officers were expecting cold beer—the NORMAL "giveaway" beverage. They reluctantly accepted the red wine, but it really didn't do much to satiate their thirst, so most of them ordered another, and another, anon.

As you might expect, the red wine was making some folks, ahh . . . sick . . . with a queasy stomach. Well, "our hero" was among the folks not feeling very good, so he decided to get some fresh air, in the hope that he would not regurgitate. As he walked down the long hall toward the exit, he noticed a very nicely dressed, prim, white-haired, "elderly" lady sitting on a wicker sofa which was surrounded by wicker chairs. She was wearing a "fancy" bright white Sun Dress, with bright red flowers all over it. He must have been staggering because she got up, walked over to him, and said, "Let me help you, son." She took his hand, and led him over to where she had been sitting, all the way speaking softly and soothingly to him.

The soothing voice of this really nice lady made him feel a lot better, but it was also making him relax and a bit sleepy. The more she cooed softly to him, the sleepier he became, and, before he knew it, he was putting his head on her lap. The minutes that followed ensured the high probability that he would be assigned an amazingly great Call Sign, which no one would <u>never</u> forget.

Sure enough, he <u>regurgitated most of his red wine</u> all over the lap of the nice lady's white sun dress with the "cute" red flowers on it!

He was so embarrassed that he bolted out the Main Door, and made a Bee Line to the BOQ (<u>B</u>achelor <u>O</u>fficers

Quarters) trying his best not to stagger (. . . . to no avail, of course).

When he sobered up, and went to work on Monday, all of his peers surrounded him, asking all kinds of questions, and laughing rather loudly. When he looked at the Ready Room Flight Schedule Board, he noticed that that his real name had been erased, and replaced with his new Call Sign: Yup! It was <u>PUKER</u>!!

Well, it took a bit longer, but he and his Commanding Officer initially did not know WHO the nice lady was who received a lap full of . . . ah . . . regurgitation, but about a week later, it was discovered that the nice lady was NOT just a nice Lady . . . . she was the WIFE of the <u>Commandant</u> <u>of the Marine Corps</u>!

Obviously, his Call Sign became, simply:

"<u>PUKER!</u>"

Chapter 15

Mike "Lancer" Sullivan
USMC

Now—let's talk about a legendary Marine Fighter Pilot:
General Mike (Lancer) Sullivan

. . . . but first, I think I need to get some readers up to speed regarding one definition

"LANCER"

A. One who carries a lance
B. A member of a military organization/unit formally composed of light cavalry with lances
C. A guy who can make you feel like a "ROOKIE" after he beats you like a drum during an Air Combat Maneuvering (ACM) sortie.

Please keep that in mind as you read this Chapter. The General has confided in me that he has "lots" of crazy stories somewhere in the back of his "Brain Housing Group," so he thought for about a New York Minute, and came up with what you are now about to read. He chose to begin in his own "formative" years.

After earning his "Wings," he was assigned to the Air Detachment at MCB (Marine Corps Base) Quantico, Virginia. While there, he received good instruction from his Senior Officers, who "brought him up." In those days, all Aviators were required to fly at least four (4) hours of First Pilot time (i.e. Meaning that the guy who actually has his hands on the stick, flight time) every month, regardless of the job to which they were assigned. Lieutenant Sullivan (among the others) knew that if they didn't get at least four (4) hours of First Pilot time on any given month, they would not get any Flight Pay for that month. Now, a cut-back in "Dollars American" really puts a dent in a Lieutenant's time at the Officers' Club Bar . . . . where the "action" is usually happening!

Accordingly, all Aviators made sure that they got their minimum of at least four (4) hours every month by the end of each month, unless they were in the hospital or dead! Otherwise, they made sure that they all flew 4+ hours EVERY MONTH, without fail. This situation also precipitated a new lexicon of words regarding Marine Aviation. One of my personal favorites is "Bagger." A "Bagger" is an aviator, who is normally found hanging around the Ready Room Desk a lot, so as to "Bag a Hop" if someone else cancels his hop for "whatever reason." (Aside: Most GOOD Operations Officers try hard to ensure that all of his aviators get access to flying machines so that his guys can get their requisite flight time. Yup. (That's why the Operations Officers would hang out at the Officers' Club Bar during the first two weeks of the month, looking for a free beer or two . . . . of course, that was years ago . . . .). I have studied this somewhat-strange ritual before in quite some detail . . . . back to the days when I was an Operations Officer, myself!

Well, Lancer and his pals worked their way through the "beer for flight time" routine ("A couple of beers a night for the Operations Officer was a pretty good deal so as to ensure that precious Flight Pay coming their way!) Lancer managed to figure that one out quite well. He and his buddies found themselves in a "Slip, Trip, and Fall" situation within two or three weeks . . . . they started dating the girls at Mary Washington College, nearby Quantico.

Lancer and his buddies decided that their new girl friends "needed" to have a real fly-over or two, or more . . . . I think you get the idea. The first Fly-Over (around dinner time) had a few girls standing on the lawn, watching. The next day they drew a few more people, and on the third day it looked as if the whole Student Body was there!

Now, <u>THAT</u> was the GOOD news! The <u>BAD</u> news was that (they didn't know it, <u>BUT</u>) . . . . there was a Retired Marine Master Sargent—and former Naval Aviator (YES, we DID have Enlisted Marine Pilots at one time!)—who was coaching the Girls' Softball Team. He had watched all three (3) flight demonstrations, and he was sure that "Those YAHOO cowboys (NOT my words) are gonna KILL themselves, and take a lot of PRETTY GIRLS with them!"

Well . . . . Since Lancer and his buddies were the ONLY Quantico Marines airborne at the same time and dates—THREE days in a ROW—it was not tough to come up with anything for an excuse better than, "Aw, Shucks! We didn't mean no harm . . . ." and, as you might guess, that turd did <u>NOT</u> float!

To finish the examination, "The Suits" (Investigation Committee) interviewed the "Guilty Bastards"—Ah, please excuse me. I meant, Marine Officers who were "selected" to go on trial—Marine style.

Then they got around to asking the Enlisted Marines who were riding in the back seats, what had <u>really</u> happened (so as to corroborate or deny what the pilots had testified). To the man, they all said that, "Nuthin' happened, Sir!" and "We weren't looking out," and "They were pulling Gs, so I must have passed out!"

Well, it turned out that one of the Grunts (Non-Pilot Marines) thought that a "G" was a "Grand" . . . . of MONEY, and NOT a measure of GRAVITY! (That didn't help HIS case at all).

When the Board finished their deliberations, they ordered all who were involved to report to the Colonel's Meeting Room. The Colonel was seated at the head of the long green table. Someone grumbled, "Oh crap! It's the Long Green Table . . . . (the one you see just before you get kicked out of the Corps!") Everyone's arm pits got soaking wet, and the Colonel hadn't even uttered a single word yet

Oddly, there were no papers of any kind in sight.

The Colonel was the first to speak. He said that he has this same problem just about every year about this time. Also, a few years ago, a Marine First Lieutenant flew up to the Washington Monument, and was playing "ring around the monument!" When he was "BUSTED, he was asked "WHY" he did it. His only response was, "Err, Brain Fart, Sir!"

No one laughed but the Colonel. Everyone else in the room was sweating like a very tired ole plow horse! He continued by saying that we (Pilots) all had done well while at TBS (The Basic School), as well as your first Gun Squadron (here), and that he realized that you all were just getting some of the pressure out of your systems, BUT that is not a proper way to be doing it . . . . <u>like you just did</u>!

Now, you all did quite well at whatever you had been doing, and for guys with just a relatively small amount of flight time, I have been told that you fly formation quite well . . . . even the ole Flying Gunny who saw you fly in formation said so. Accordingly, here is what I am going to do. <u>ATTENTION TO ORDERS!</u>

1. All of you WILL get a <u>VERBAL</u> <u>WARNING</u> from me, and
2. I "<u>may</u>" make calls to your new COs in the Fleet, to ensure that they know what they are getting. <u>IF,</u> of course . . . . I can <u>remember</u> to call them.

Any questions?

No? . . . . and with just a moment's pause, he barked <u>DISMISSED</u>!!

WHAT?

That's <u>IT</u>?

They all thought as they marched out. This is exactly what we all <u>wanted</u> to happen . . . . but none of us thought it would ever actually happen.

Walking out the door, I took a quick look back into the Board Room. The Colonel already had his feet on the long green tablecloth, and was lighting a big cigar!

From that time, EVERYTHING seemed to go a whole lot easier and smoother, for <u>all of us</u>

Chapter 16

"Gerber" to "Magic"
<u>USMC</u>

<u>Item A</u>

After having earned my Naval Aviator "Wings" I was assigned to MCAS (<u>M</u>arine <u>C</u>orps <u>A</u>ir <u>S</u>tation), Cherry Point, at Havelock, North Carolina for further training. Upon arrival, I reported to the Air Wing, and was further reassigned to the Air Group, which, at the time, was composed of three (3) Training Squadrons: One for A-4s, one for A-6s, and one for F-4s, plus other support squadrons. I was ordered to immediately check in at the Air Group, then the Group Operations Officer, who immediately pointed me to the Group Training Officer—(Then) Captain John Church (The "Silver Fox") and THIS fox actually <u>did</u> have silver hair).

As soon as I talked to Captain Church, I instinctively realized that he was, indeed, a great guy, and Leader of Marines as well. Without ado, he told me that I had been assigned to the A-6 Training squadron.

I was shocked!

I had been told when I left the Naval Air Training Command, the Senior Marine (a Full Bird Colonel) said that I would be reporting into the F-4 squadron at Cherry Point, due in the most part, because of my top-of-the-class performance in the Training Command (and it was right there—in black and white—in my Orders, as well).

Well, it turned out that Captain Church was an F-4 RIO (Radar Intercept Officer), and he immediately felt my pain . . . . so he was willing to try to make a deal.

After a long discussion, he said, "OK. Here's the Game Plan: I will try to turn things around at my level, and upward, but YOU will also need to work it from your end, as well—BUT do not bother to tell anyone else that we are working this together, or I will be sent to the Salt Mines, and you will get assigned to flying helicopters in Fairbanks Alaska!" Hmm . . . . THAT was language I could understand! Unfortunately, when I left his office I was very down-trodden, yet hopeful that we could turn things around.

A couple of weeks later, after I received that shot of cold urine to the heart, my wife and I went to Church on Base. I happened to notice a very "squared-away" Two Star General, with silver-grey hair a few pews in front of us. His hair was cut "high and tight" . . . . but I casually mentioned to my wife that the General really had his "act" together (but . . . . in actuality, I didn't use the word "act."

After church, we drove to the Officers' Club for lunch. The Club was packed with Marine Officers and their wives. Although we had to wait for a table, we were seated in reasonably short order. Shortly after we sat down, a waiter inquired if we would mind having two more folks at the table, and we said, "Certainly! That would be fine!"

Well, lo and behold, it was the General that we saw in church, with his wife. (I must admit that this was a pretty big event for my wife and I. We had never shared a table with a Two Star General . . . . or any other General, for that manner!)

The discussions at the table were relaxed (Well, as relaxed as a First Lieutenant could possibly be with a 2-Star General at the same table). The General's wife and my wife got along splendidly, and the General kept the conversation going along nicely with me . . . . well, until he asked me, "So, which Squadron are you in?

Well, I felt my palms start to get sweaty and surmised that I was currently at one of those, "Pick the horse you think is the best one, and RIDE IT" situations, so I very politely said, "Well, Sir, I was just recently assigned to the A-6 Training

Squadron, while looking the General, eye-to-eye. The General thought for just a moment, then looking me right in the eye, said "Is that what you REALLY want to do?"

WOW! He must have been a super "FACE Reader!"

For a moment, I went blank, simply because I didn't know if I could say what I really WANTED to say, especially to a Two Star General . . . . Well, the General didn't rise to be a General by being dumb, so he jumped right on me. "What's the matter, Lieutenant? What's on your mind?"

"Well, thank you, General!" is what I was saying to myself, so, I tried to lower the tone of my voice, took a deep breath, and said, "Well, Sir, I joined the Marine Corps to be a Fighter Pilot. I worked very hard in the Training Command, so as to be at the top of my class, so that I could BE a fighter pilot. However, I was very recently told that I am now slotted to become an A-6 pilot, although I have worked my BUTT OFF to be a Fighter Pilot. Please excuse me if I might sound like a whiner, Sir, but that was why I worked so hard for, during the past two years."

The next thing I saw was him standing up. I rose quickly from the table, immediately stood up with him, and snapped into the position of Attention.

At that moment I realized that I lost ANY chance, whatsoever, of becoming a Fighter Pilot. However—to my great surprise, he began to laugh . . . . LOUDLY!

Then he said, "Don't you worry about THAT, son. I want you to report to the Air Group Commander, himself, on Monday morning. In the meantime, I will make a few calls, and get those guys squared away! OK?"

Of course, I said, "YES, SIR! OK, and THANK you, SIR!"

The next day, I put on my perfectly put-together Alpha Uniform, with my brass and shoes shining brightly, and reported to the Group Commander at exactly 0800 (Eight O'Clock), sharp.

The Group Commander wasted no time. "You have a lot of nerve! You went over my head, and told the General that you want to be a Fighter Pilot. Is that correct?"

"Yes, Sir!"

I tried to bark back in my most military voice, but it only came out as a "whimper" of sorts. "The General ordered me to report to you at the first thing this morning, Sir!"

He was quick to reply, "Well, I don't like people who go behind my back, but based on my "One Way" conversation with the General this morning, it has become obvious that I have to do something about this. Accordingly, I now have to find room for you in my RF-4 (a reconnaissance version of the F-4) squadron, so as to comply with the Boss' order. I understand that you profess that you want to be a Fighter Pilot. Is that true?

A loud "Yes, Sir" came out of my mouth before I even thought about it.

He said, "So tell me one good reason why I should let you to try to become a <u>real</u> fighter pilot?

This was a very important question for me, and I <u>HAD</u> to get it right, so I hesitated for just a moment, and then said "Sir, I joined the Marine Corps to <u>KILL</u> people, NOT to take <u>PICTURES</u> of them!

The Colonel's eyes opened wide, and then he broke into a belly laugh, and said, "Son—that's the best answer I have heard in a very long time! May I use that line?"

I answered, "Yes, Sir! BUT, it's <u>NOT</u> a "line" Sir."

He laughed even louder!

So, that's how I became an F-4 pilot.

A <u>FIGHTER</u> <u>PILOT</u>! That was a <u>REALLY</u> big deal!

Item B

"Gerber"

After an eight month assignment to VMFA-513, flying F-4Bs at MCAS Cherry Point, the Squadron was selected to be the first AV-8B squadron, so I received orders to MCAS, Beaufort, South Carolina, along with several other Fighter/ Attack drivers. When we got there, the Admin Officer (Whom I supposed to be an F-4 pilot) said "We've already got the word on you, boy." Pause. Pause . . . . (just waiting for a "barb" from him). "Oh, yeah! We need some feisty guys like you to fly OUR jets!" You could have heard my sigh of relief all the way out in the parking lot!

So I was assigned to my first true "Gun" Squadron—VMFA-251—a very highly decorated unit. A unit to which I was fortunate to be assigned for a total of three times in my career! Iconic senior Marines of the "Do it right the first time, every time!" school of thought were my mentors. They led me and other fledglings to learn and retain the ability to "deliver the "mail" through the Ashau Valley." (A VERY nasty, area in South East Asia.)

Aside: When it was my turn to deliver the "Mail" (Read BOMBS) to the Ashau Valley (ON the "bad guys), I did it with great gusto because:

1) I wanted to live another day . . . . and
2) To do it again the next day, etc, etc!

It was always a great RUSH! We "youngsters" were very fortunate to have many "survivors" of the conflict, who became our mentors.

Most of them went "In Country," did "their thing," and returned to the "States" with a deep and wide breadth of knowledge about defeating the Bad Guys. Most of them would/did volunteer to go back again, and again (until someone in Washington realized what they were doing), and plugged up those possibilities. Simply said: Those guys quickly became our Heroes!

As was the custom back in the 60's, Friday night was always reserved for the Squadron Pilots and RIOs (Radar Intercept Officers, who flew in the back seat of the F-4) to get together and listen to the "Sea Stories" of our "Elders" who had "been there and done that!" In the squadron at that time, we had a lot of, untested youngsters, such as myself, so we tried real hard to learn everything and anything we could from the experienced gents.

One Friday night we had a Squadron party at "Toad Hall"—a World War Two Quonset Hut (Just imagine a really BIG roll of toilet paper—with no toilet paper on it something akin to corrugated steel/tin), about 20 feet wide and 60 feet long. Three of our Squadron Mates (all bachelors, of course) lived there. It turned out to be the "PERFECT Party House!"

They chose to call it "Toad Hall". (Think about it . . . .)

I chose not to tell any of the wives how they chose to dub it . . . . let's just say that the guys didn't go out with too many "Glamor Girls."

When my wife and I arrived, the party was already in full swing, and—since I was one of the lowly "new" Lieutenants to join the Squadron—I was ordered to accompany Earl (The Squirrel) Hailston—another "new guy" in the Squadron, to go to a store and get an "adequate amount" of beer.

(Definition: An "<u>ADEQUATE</u>" amount of beer in the Marine Corps (in those days) was as much cold beer as two well-muscled, in great shape, Rocket Scientist Marines (who, preferably, have a Pick-Up truck) with an un-fettered amount of Dollars-American can buy within a reasonable amount of time.)

Well, Earl and I took up a collection from everyone, and we were off.

After piling up as much beer as we thought we could carry/ push in two carts, we toted our "precious cargo" toward the cashier. As we walked through food aisles, Earl stopped his cart and put down the beers he was hand carrying. He went over to the Baby Food Section, picked up a jar of baby food, held it up next to my cheek, and starting yelling, "New Call Sign! New Call Sign!"

Well, what he had in his hand was a jar of "Gerber" Baby Food, with—of course—the Gerber Baby on the label. I immediately told him that I would beat him like a dusty rug if he did that to me—we were standing nose-to-nose during this . . . ah . . . conversation. Well, he laughed, and I thought I saw him return the jar to the shelf. Well, we then paid for the beer and he somehow stuffed it away in the bed of the truck, and took it back to "Toad Hall," and we distributed the beer among our Squadron Mates and Ladies.

I thought the "Gerber" episode was over, but—a minute later—Earl pulled another bottle of baby food out of his jacket pocket, and continued his rampage of, "<u>LOOK</u>! <u>ITS GERBER</u>!" . . . . over, and over, until I grabbed him . . . . but the damage had already been done. How in the world did I get into this mess ?

Our C.O. (LtCol Rocky Plant) came over to me a few minutes later, put his arm around my shoulder (like he was going to be "nice" to me) and said, "Ya know, Lieutenant, in all the years I've been flying, I never actually knew of <u>anybody</u> who used "<u>Gerber</u>" as a Call Sign!! HA HA!"

Well, if he wasn't my Commanding Officer, who would write and submit my Performance Evaluations, and a well-known and <u>very</u> good Middle-Weight professional boxer prior to joining the Corps, with a Call Sign of <u>Rocky,</u> I would have just kicked his ass!

YEAH <u>SURE</u>!

Soon after that I got my call to ship out to West Pac.

I was prepared to "do my thing with serious hopes that "Gerber" would soon just go away.

Shortly after my arrival in Iwakuni, Japan, my new squadron (VMFA-232: Red Devils) was ordered to immediately deploy to Da Nang airfield in South Viet Nam. "Well, all right! I am going In-Country!"

Unfortunately, my elation did NOT last long, because about two hours after we landed at Da Nang the sun went down, and our Squadron endured our first "Welcome Aboard" rocket attack. The first rocket that hit the ground got me straight up from my cot! The second one got me on the deck . . . . and the third one convinced me that we needed some kind of shelter!

Well, I got my wish for a shelter when I got up the next morning. About only 40 yards from our hooch was a BIG and DEEP crater. That's a REAL BIG and REAL DEEP hole! Ah, did I tell you it was big and deep? That didn't scare ME much . . . . OH, NO!

Now, the GOOD news was that our "Hootch" now had a shelter to jump into during rocket attacks. The BAD news was that they could possibly lob another one in the same hole! (The "real" truth was that they couldn't hit a target with those rockets unless the target was as big as-say, an Air Base. So, mathematically, we didn't have to worry. You know: "The odds were in our favor!" That's my story, and I'm sticking to it! (Aside: What ELSE could we do?)

At breakfast, the CO came over and sat across the table from me, and immediately said, "Gerber, you're the Safety Nazi, right?"

I replied, "Yes, Sir!"

He said, "Good. I want those rockets to go away. Fix it . . . It's a SAFETY responsibility, that's an order, Captain, and, by the way, DFIU!"

I think I automatically switched to the "deer in the headlights" mode.

Well, that was a pretty well-received joke through-out the Squadron. Even the "Troops" knew about it, and wanted to know when I was going to get "my job" done! It was actually a pretty good morale booster for most of the Squadron, because it took everyone's mind off all the "other" things they were worried about.

Rather than just sit around, I "sniveled" a day off the Flight Schedule so as to go over to see the Air Force Intelligence guys on the other side of the runway, to see if they could give me a good "local tactical assessment" brief. When they were done, I asked "What would happen if I took a Platoon of Marines up there in the hills, and killed them all? That would end our problem, right?

They laughed!

Here's how it works, Captain: An "expendable person" (who just came out of a rice paddy for the first time in his/her life) is given a single, rather heavy rocket to be strapped on his/her back, and told to take it to the top of the hill at Da Nang. They get there in about a month if everything goes "well" (by their standards). They turn over the rocket to someone there on the mountain, and he says "Thank You. Go back and get me another one."

So, I said, "OK. I guess I understand that, but why don't we just let me take a Platoon of our Jar Heads up there, and wipe them off the face of the earth?

"Ah, so," they responded. "If we did that, they might send down some people from Hanoi who <u>are</u> <u>smart</u> <u>enough</u> to launch those rockets <u>ACCURATELY</u>!"

Hmmm, I couldn't think of anything to say, so I just said, "Never mind!"

TAKE AWAY: "It is never as easy as it would seem to be on the first try."

At Da Nang, we had two USMC Squadrons (1 F-4J and 1 F-4B), and four or five USAF F-4 Squadrons (rotational), along with Air Force Jolly Green Giants (Rescue Choppers with USAF Special Operations personnel on board), Air Force A-1s to lead the "Jollies" to find the guy (or guys) on the ground, and apply firepower where/when required and/or desired). The Air Force also had "Puff the Magic Dragon" a C-117 converted into a "Gun Ship" which had several high-caliber machine guns as well as a 105mm cannon, and several other "toys" to get the "Bad Guys Attention.

We also had a B-52 that "zigged" when they should have "zagged," while engaged on a mission "Up North," and got

HIT . . . . <u>Big</u> <u>Time!</u> They had lost two engines on the outboard Port side—WHOOPS—I meant on the <u>LEFT</u> side for the USAF folks! I had the great honor of watching the wounded B-52 perform the dreaded "<u>Six Engine Approach</u>" into Da Nang!

For over a week, we had the "honor" of having that B52 sitting on the tarmac about 500 feet away from our hooch. That single B-52 attracted <u>at least</u> a dozen rockets or more <u>every</u> night for several nights. Our Squadron's "Hooch" was about 100 yards from where the "BUF" (<u>B</u>ig <u>U</u>gly FxxxxR) was parked—and the Bad Guys' rockets were NOT accurate weapons—so, to say that we were "concerned" would be a <u>REAL</u> under-statement! Nothing personal, of course, to you Air Force guys out there, but we were sure glad when you got your BUFF (known by our Marines In Country, as the "Rocket Magnet) <u>OUT</u> of Da Nang!

For almost a week, we had the "honor" of betting amongst ourselves when the NVA "target practice" finally "took out" that BUF. It would have been a sad day for the Marine Corps, as well, because if one of those yo-yos actually HIT the B-52, a whole lot of us wouldn't be here writing or reading this book today!

After an "eternity" of sitting on our ramp, the BUF fired up its engines, taxied out, and successfully took off on its way to any place but <u>Da Nang</u>! No one shed a tear.

Well, we wanted to do something "special" in celebration of the BUF's departure, so a few of us went over to the "No Hob" Club.

NOTE: So as to ease some of the pain of living at Da Nang, the US Air Force chose to allow an indigenous merchant to open a restaurant, on site, which would morph into a Bar at night. This establishment was dubbed the "No Hob Club." When you enter, you see a huge bar and smaller tables around, butted up to the walls. Plaques with Menu choices were hung high on the walls ALL THE WAY AROUND THE ROOM! Wow! What a menu!—there must have been <u>forty</u> or more entrees! GREAT!

The Bar Tender came up to us and said, "What yo hab, sar?"

I said Budweiser Beer, please, and my buddy said, "I'll have the same."

The Bartender said, "OK, GI!"

As he went for the beer, we looked at the menu. I wanted a bowl of Chili, to start. My buddy thought that was a good idea, as well, so when the bartender came back with the beers, he asked us, "Yoe eat?"

I replied, "Sure! Two bowls of Number 46, Chili, please."

He said, "No Hob."

Hmmm—OK, let's look at the menu again. "How about Number 37—two Hot Dogs?"

He said, "No Hob."

We were both just a little warm under the collar, thinking that he was mocking us, however we were "guests" in <u>his</u> Country, so we "did it <u>his</u> way" for about three more tries. By this time we were getting more than just a little bit—ahh—perturbed? So, without thinking I raised my voice, and said, "So, what <u>DO</u> you have?"

With a great big smile on his face, he said, "Hamburga! Cheburga! Dis No Hob Club. We No Hob no ding baat Humburga an Cheesburga!" We cracked up, and my buddy almost fell off his bar stool, laughing, without even having a "sniff" of beer yet!

A <u>GREAT</u> TIME was had by ALL! We also brought our Squadron Mates to the No Hob Club—one by one—and let them order anything on all the boards in the place. It was an absolute HOOT watching them!

PS: I think that might have been the funniest thing I ever saw while at DaNang or anywhere else we went in South-East Asia!

ITEM C

Redemption

Upon my return to the Good Ole USA, I was stationed at MCAS Beaufort, South Carolina, just up the road from Marine Corps Recruit Center, Parris Island. I was assigned to an F-4 Gun Squadron for about two years, until I was informed that it was "my turn in the barrel" to serve as a member of the Marine Air Group Staff (MAG-31). I must admit that—at first—I really missed those close relationships that only a good Squadron can offer, but there were lots of good, competent folks at the Group as well, and I started thinking at a little higher and wider perspective (which was exactly why the Marine Corps assigns their potential leaders in that very manner).

While several of us moved to the Group staff, we were still allowed to fly with the "Gun Squadrons" in order to keep our "currency" in the F-4, just in case "something happened." We also had the opportunity to fly the Group's TA-4s (dual-seated A-4s—AKA: Scooters) which were predominately used as "Aggressors" for the F-4 Squadrons, and for "proficiency" flying for the Group Staff. I found that the TA-4 is a pretty neat airplane to fly—especially in the Air-To-Air roll. The TA-4 turns "on a dime," and could—if flown properly and aggressively—do a lot of damage to a poorly-flown F-4. As the Assistant Operations Officer at the Group Headquarters,

I was ordered to pull together a formal plan/system to support the Group's F-4 Squadrons' MCRES (Marine Corps Readiness Evaluation System) testing evolution.

Once I got that ball into the air with the F-4 Squadrons, among the first things that I did was to sign up to personally participate, and then find the best pilot I could find to go flying with me.

Finding the best pilot was really simple—I just called Larry "Stick" Richards, who, had just arrived at MCAS Beaufort a few weeks prior, who previously was a Top Gun Instructor Pilot at and a MIG Killer while flying in combat with the Air Force.

We quickly flew a few ACM (Air Combat Maneuvering) sorties together at MCAS Beaufort, and then flew our "Little Grey Fighter" out to MCAS Yuma, in South West Arizona. Our initial job there was to get the deployed Group F-4J Fighter Squadron up to their best possible capabilities, prior to their participating in the MCRES.

We—among many others—worked hard to get the F-4s up to snuff where they needed to be, specifically on the Air-To-Air part of the MCRES. They called us their "Bubbas" for the Air-To-Air portions. From the first day, we knew that they had done their preparations and "studies" quite well, and—in our professional opinions, we felt pretty sure that they would do very well. We were flying as many ACM (<u>A</u>ir <u>C</u>ombat <u>M</u>aneuvering) hops as we could. The USMC Phantoms also knew what they needed to work on, and how to do it correctly. The "Game Plan" was moving along, and looking good!

When it came time for the "joust," the Air Force came to MCAS Yuma "to teach the Marines a lesson or two" for the Final Event—The Air to Air "show down." The USAF showed up with their (then) new "Lizard <u>Green</u>" camouflage paint job on their Phantoms. (Hmmm—the best color for a Fighter maneuvering over a light tan desert floor should be light tan, so as to fit in with the extant topography). We made it a point to mention that fact to the CO of <u>our</u> Gun Squadron. Our other recommendation to "our" F-4s was to: Fly to the "merge" <u>high</u>, but below the contrail altitude, and look <u>DOWN</u> at the green gobblers (USAF F-4s) on the light tan background of the desert." (We got several cold beers for sharing that thought with "Our Boys" at the bar that night.)

The "happening" on the next day was quite a gaggle! The sky was full of green (bad guys) and grey (good guys) turning and twisting to beat the band! The Marines did well, but were not perfect—yet! On the second day, they were a LOT better, and on the third day they even allowed us, in our "little ole two hole A-4," join in the fun, and "run with the big boys!"

We decided that our best plan would be to stay out of the way of the of the Phantoms on the way to the "merge" and shoot a "cripple" or a clueless "Green Jet" who had his head up his—ahhh—posterior. Well, it turned out to be a really BIG GAGGLE!

It was <u>GREAT</u>!

We quickly found ourselves cutting inside a turning "Green" F-4 who was trying hard to glom-on to one of "our" F-4s, and so I got a great "Growl" (signifying that the Sidewinder had locked on the hot shot in front of me), took a "Heater" (Sidewinder) shot, and called it in to the "Bunker." We reversed to the right after we shot, and—WOW!—there was another one, driving along in full-burner right across our nose, just as Stick called "Break Right NOW, HIGH," so I did, and watched a another green F-4 streak past us, at the speed of "stink," so I shot him, with a Sidewinder, as well! "Stick commented that, "You're not being FAIR with these "Air Force" guys, ya know?

I said, "Did <u>YOU</u> ever play fair?"

(Note: Have you ever tried to laugh out loud when you are pulling 5-6 Gs?)

It might not have been true, but I thought all of the "Green" F-4s must have had a plan to fly in front of our "Little Gray Fighter." Stick was more pragmatic—"Quit bitchin'! You might not ever see something like this again!" Since I had the "pedal to the metal" throughout the entire fight, I took a peek at the gas gauge, and—yup—we were a wee bit below our "Bug Out" fuel estimate, so it was time for us to turn our nose toward Yuma.

Not surprisingly, just about everyone else seemed to be heading back to Yuma, as well (for the same reason—FUEL). As I turned West "Stick" barked out, "Hard port, high, right to left, bad guys!" Before he stopped talking, I was pointing our nose to the South, looking high. As they flew over us, they were still in the Warning Area, and no one had said "Knock it off" yet over the radios, so, accordingly, the "Fight" was still on," so . . . . we shot them both! A few seconds later we heard, words to the effect of, "Scooter kill! . . . . Make that TWO kills!" Hmm . . . . Stick said, "That wasn't real pretty, but it's a pair of kills!"

As we were starting to descend on the way to Home plate, I "just happened" to look into my Port mirror, and saw two MORE (2) Green F-4s in Loose Deuce, hauling "butt," at my 8:00, so I pulled straight up, slowly rolled over toward them, and—again—they didn't see us. I asked, "Is the fight still on?" and got an immediate "Roger" from the "Bunker." <u>OK!</u>

So, we just pulled a little power and dropped down on the guy on the right, shot, and then slid to the left "participant", and heard the "Bunker" report "Kill," and "Kill!"

All we could say was "WOW!"

After landing, we shut down, and our little Second Lieutenant "controller," came running over to the bottom of our ladder. He was acting crazy, and had a grin in his face that went from ear to ear! The very first thing that he said was, "You Guys were great out there today!" Blah, Blah. WOW! Blah, Blah! WOW . . . .

We both politely said "Thanks. Let's de-brief right here, before we go over to the Officers' Club for the Mass De-Briefing. During our Trio De-Brief, it was then revealed to us that we had been credited for SIX kills on that mission (I thought we got 5, and so did "Stick.) Hmmm, should we argue? NAH!

The three of us headed for the O-Club for the "Mass Debriefing," with our youngster in-tow. When we got there, we were told that the Commanding Officer in charge of the USAF side of the Exercise had canceled the Mass Debrief because the USMC F-4s (. . . . and one little ole TA-4) had taken them to the "wood shed!" Their CO was so irate and embarrassed that, instead of staying over-night (as per their initial plan), he ordered that his jets be filled with gas, and flown home IMMEDIATELY!

After hearing that, we realized that Right There—was <u>gonna be the best possible debrief of all time</u>!

The USMC De-Brief was a <u>HOOT</u>! Just about everyone got at least one shot, and the Kill Ratio was way off the charts! The Senior USMC Officer In Charge Of The Exercise dismissed the audience, and invited all Marines to join him at the bar at the Officers' Club. As you might have guessed, he didn't have to ask twice!

We were a bit surprised when we got to the Club, and discovered that the noise was <u>WAY up there</u>, and there was already about an inch of "liquid?" and beer all over the floor around the bar. Our 2nd Lieutenant's eyes were as big as Goose Eggs! To him, it wasn't "the FAST lane, NO! . . . . It was the <u>SUPERSONIC</u> lane!"

As we waded through the masses—all jammed together "in rear-ends to belly buttons"—to get to the bar. We noted that one of the beer kegs had <u>already</u> been killed. While I was pouring a beer at the bar, for our "Controller," he yelled in my ear, and told me that a "Bird Colonel" across the room was pointing at you . . . . I looked across the room . . . . it was then Colonel Mike (Lancer) Sullivan (the Officer In

Charge of the Exercise). He beckoned us to come over to him. I really wanted to hear what he had to say about the day's happenings, so the three of us slopped though a sea of people and beer, over to the Colonel.

When we got there, he had a big/wide grin on his face. The Colonel (Lancer) just about broke the bones in my hand when I shook his hand. "Stick" got the same reception. Lancer thought our "performance" was great! He ascertained that we scored five (5) kills, and couldn't get over the fact that we could "lift our legs just as high as the BIG dogs could" (Meaning the F-4s) vs our little ole, sub-sonic "Scooter.")

I suppose that we were talking real loud, and none of us were giving much attention to our young "Controller," so he must have felt that he ought to say "something" for the "good of the club," so he blurted out, "Yes, SIR! He was absolutely MAGIC out there today, Sir!"

I cringed a bit, but Lancer cracked up! Then he said "Well . . . . that's sure a better Call Sign for you than "Gerber" . . . . "MAGIC"!

And so, Gerber simply faded away, never to be seen nor heard again . . . . and I was HAPPY!

P.S. General Lancer, after all these years, I <u>still</u> think that it was GREAT for you to get rid of "Gerber" for me!

I remain indebted to you, Sir . . . .

Semper Fi,

Magic